MISTY GIANTS OF THE LAVA BEDS

BIGFOOT STORIES FROM THE NASS VALLEY

DR. MITCH VERDE, PHD

CONTENTS

PREFACE

Dr. Mitch Verdehl way, ii Phd Psychology niiy. Nisga'a niiy, Laxgibuu niiy, ii Wilps Duuḵ'. Laxgalts'ap wil jogay. Tankers Road wil witgwiy. Gordon McKayhl was niye'e, ii Salome McKayhl was nijiits. Carlos Verdehl was nigwoodiy, ii Bernice Verdehl was nooy. Larry Erickson was my dad. Baxt'aahl was Nisga'a.

My name is Dr. Mitch Verde, and I hold a PhD in Psychology. I am a member of the Nisga'a First Nation. I am from one of the wolf tribes, and I come from the House of Duuḵ'. My family comes from Laxgalts'ap, and I live on Tankers Road in the Nass Valley. Gordon and Salome McKay were my grandparents, and Carlos and Bernice Verde are the names of my biological parents. Larry Erickson is my dad. My Nisga'a name is Baxt'aa. This introduction is the traditional way that Nisga'a people introduce themselves.

Humans are social and curious creatures. As a result, they relay their curiosity and wonderment of the natural world through stories and storytelling. All cultures value storytelling...they tell of our creation and lived experiences, and some stories are created to describe and attribute meaning to things we do not understand. I decided to write this book twelve years ago. I had a simple plan for the book to present the experiences of people I had met who claimed to have seen Bigfoot or knew someone who had experienced Bigfoot. I also wanted to present my personal experiences with Bigfoot and describe some of the psychology related to the Bigfoot phenomena.

1

INTRODUCTION

When I started this book, I held a master's degree in psychology and worked in the mental health field, and later, I worked as a college professor. I understood that the single biggest problem that leads to problems in thinking is how we think about problems. Philosophy shows us that problems can be approached through the use of logic. Psychology has made links between attention, emotions, thoughts, beliefs, and behavior. Logically, if those links exist, then individuals, based on their experiential history, 'should' be creating subjective realities. We then share our subjective realities and find common ground with others. One result is that two or more camps can emerge on different sides of an issue. It could be that the truth lies somewhere in between, is more weighted towards one perspective than the others, or is completely one-sided. One concern with logic is that you require accurate knowledge of the premise of a phenomenon before logic is useful as a thinking structure for determining truth. Psychology has its own problems, particularly in making the leap from basic research findings in the lab to accounting for complex human experiences in the real world. However, as a human species, we do not systematically teach ways of thinking that are reality-based, and this is causing us great problems.

Time is a great balancer of subjective realities. I will use a two-camp model to illustrate my point. The subjective reality camps are on either end of a teeter-totter, and all things being equal will remain suspended in the air. Time, however, has the effect of allowing people to gather evidence, which necessarily adds weight to one subjective reality. As a result, their end of the teeter-totter is lowered. When irrefutable evidence is gathered, their feet hit the ground, and an objective reality is attained for all of us to share. Whether we all accept the reality is irrelevant, as the same things that distort our perceptions, leading to problems, continue to exist in our subjective realities despite irrefutable evidence. Since I started writing this book, there were things out there in the Bigfoot discussion that have since been shown to be inaccurate. For example, a human female named Zana had been captured in Russia some years back, and she had children with some of the local men. Her mannerisms and appearance made some believe she was a female Bigfoot. In addition, one of her offspring was said to be tall and abnormally strong and had a pronounced brow ridge. In recent years, descendants of her offspring had their DNA tested, and the tests came back as modern humans. Moreover, their mitochondrial DNA indicated that Zana was actually of African descent, which would more than account for the locals' interpretation of her appearance and behavior.

During that same time, people presented information suggesting that the Bigfoot phenomenon is far stranger than I initially thought. In addition, I have documented more local eye witness sightings and experiences, as well as having many more of my own. Eight years ago, I decided to return to university to attain a PhD in psychology. I put this book on hold while I finished my doctoral degree. Two days after the final submission of my dissertation, I started writing this book again. I decided that it would be best if I used this opportunity to tell a story comprised of stories. I learned from writing my dissertation that I needed to be a bigger part of this story, not only through my own accounts but also through the lens of my culture and psychology. Like any story, I will jump around and fill in pieces that help certain things make sense. So then...this is the beginning of my story.

My name is Domingos McKay Verde, but I go by Mitch. I was nick-named after the doctor who delivered me in Prince Rupert many moons ago. I am a member of the Nisga'a First Nation, whose traditional territory is located within the Nass Valley, British Columbia (BC). I hail from the Clan of the Gitwilnak'il (The People of the One). We are one of the wolf tribes in the Nass Valley. I come from the House of Duuk̲', and from the sub-House of Gwingyoo. My Nisga'a name is Bax̲t'aa, which refers to a story of a white wolf that patrolled the cut-banks overlooking the Nass River, watching for intruders. That area where the river once flowed was moved by a lava flow caused by a volcanic eruption approximately 300 years ago. That was the last volcano to erupt in Canada. Those lava beds are the ones that are referred to in the title of this book.

When I was six years old, it was deemed by others that I was old enough to watch a particular movie at the theatre: *The Legend of Boggy Creek*. Whoever's subjective reality informed the decision that I was old enough to watch the movie was warped (it was the 70's, go figure). Although terrifying for a little tyke, there seemed to be a quality of truth to it for me, even though I had never heard of a

Bigfoot or Sasquatch before. When I was ten years old, I was cutting across an apple orchard in the BC Okanagan to get to school. As I walked under one of the trees, I looked down, and in a muddy patch of ground was an enormous human-shaped footprint. For those of you who watched the *Legend of Boggy Creek,* you might recall the young boy running across fields trying to get somewhere before it got dark (that was the scariest part of the movie for me). Well, I looked around, and there were no other tracks. It wasn't getting dark, and the road was only about three hundred feet away. I didn't run, but I did walk directly to the road and made my way to school. I didn't tell anyone but never cut across that orchard again. As I grew older, I became more aware of the Bigfoot phenomenon. However, I was in the same place as most people in that I had not seen one, and science had not cataloged one. However, science is a process. To illustrate a personal example, when I was seven years old, our family was taking a drive through the northern end of the Nass Valley. The Nass Valley is heavily wooded, and all the roads were gravel back then. We normally hunted when we traveled; most animals were on the menu. During this one trip, my brother hollered, "bear." My grandfather hit the brakes and looked over to where my brother had seen the bear, but it had moved off into the forest. My brother then said it was a polar bear because it was white. Everyone started laughing because polar bears do not live in the Nass Valley. My brother was adamant that the bear was white, and he cried because of the ridicule. Well, what he saw was not a polar bear, but in parts of the coastal forest of BC, there exists a white-colored black bear, known as a Kermode or 'Spirit Bear.' When I was young, no one had ever described seeing this color of black bear before in the Nass Valley, but now they are quite common. An outdoorsman from Minnesota came to the Nass Valley about ten years ago, and I took him on a drive about. He was incredulous when I told him about the white-black bears, and he thought I was pulling his leg. That was until we came around a corner, and this rather large Kermode bear was standing on the road eating clover. I had to rev up my engine and make several mock charges at the bear until finally after ten minutes, he moved his body off of the narrow logging road. The bear continued eating clover, and the Minnesotan ate crow.

When I was fourteen years old, I read a magazine article discussing the existence of Bigfoot and aliens. Although I can't recall the gist of the article, I did firmly conclude that I would rather have a run-in with an alien than a Bigfoot. Bigfoot still terrified me because of "that movie" and the media's portrayal of Bigfoot. Television programs and stories in books and on the internet often portray peoples' experiences with Bigfoot as terrifying encounters. As you progress through this book, I hope to help you gain a more balanced perspective on this phenomenon. I want to set the stage for those stories by discussing what I will be presenting to you.

As you read this book, you are likely a member of one of three camps of people: believers, disbelievers, and folks on fences. As the author of this book, I can unequivocally state that I am not a believer in the creature that is colloquially called "Bigfoot." I can also unequivocally state that I am not a believer in Bigfoot because I am a knower of this creature. While this is a big shoe to drop so early on, I ask that you bear with me and keep an open mind.

In this book, I am going to cover some different areas of this subject. As I indicated, one of the areas that I will be discussing is a psychological perspective. Interestingly, many of the Skeptics concerning Bigfoot re-hash arguments against the existence of Bigfoot using psychological-based theories. In addition, they do so with such exuberance and finality that one might conclude that they have a firm grasp of how sensory systems work and how the brain processes stimuli and converts them into consciousness. If it is so easy to be an armchair psychologist, why did I go to university for half of my adult life? With that in mind, I must admit to some guilt for having done the same thing over and over again. Like most of you, I try to take a balanced approach to examining evidence regarding any phenomenon, including Bigfoot. The problem is that we don't have a collectively agreed-upon reference point for informing our opinions. Some people rely on a personal experience. Some people reference the historical contacts between Indigenous Peoples and Bigfoot. Others cite the contact between European settlers and Bigfoot. Skeptics argue that we don't have a specimen, which is the only scientific proof they will accept. All of these perspectives have merit. However, there is only one truth: That the Bigfoot species exists or it does not.

Before I continue, I wanted to clarify why I chose the term Bigfoot over other terms. First, the term Bigfoot is colorful, physically descriptive, and over time, it has become a comfortable and recognizable generic name. Secondly, words such as Sasquatch and other Indigenous terms refer to creatures found in specific Indigenous territories. The names that Indigenous people use for Bigfoot are also descriptive and often reference their experiences, such as "giant", "hairy man or woman", "wild", and "land or forest."

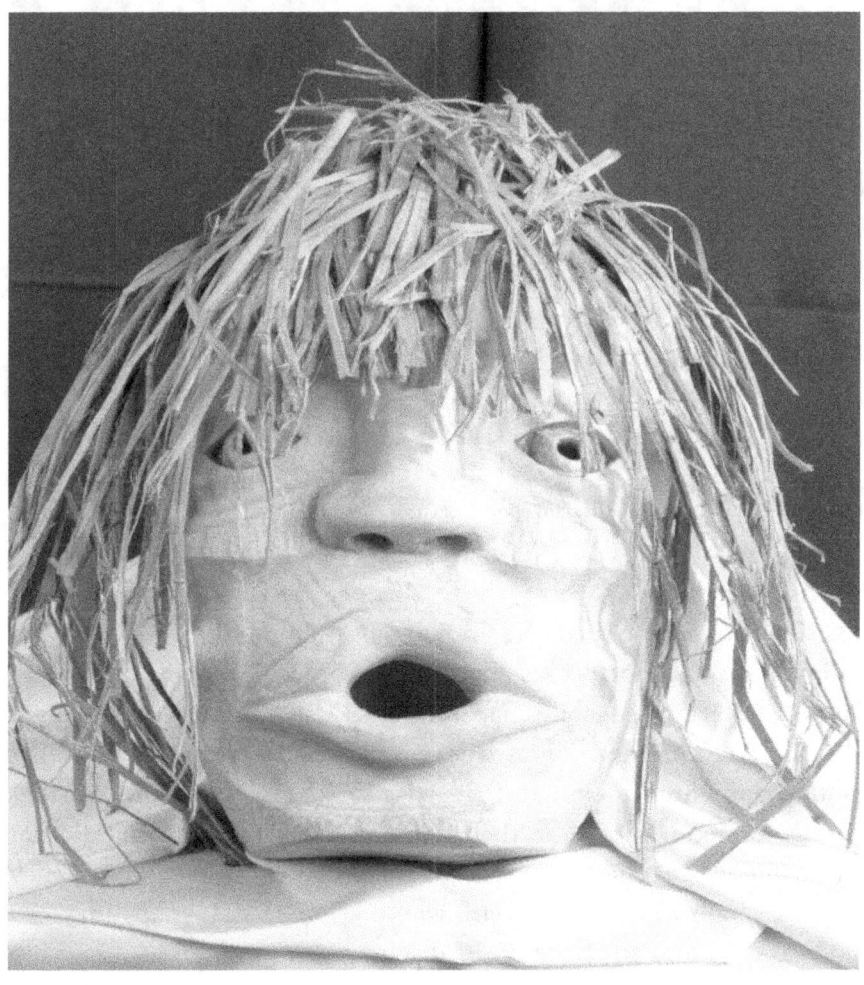

In BC, there are over thirty distinct language groups. Early missionaries catalogued the Indigenous names of the plants and animals on the north-coast of British Columbia. While there was some similarity between what different First Nations groups called the Bigfoot, different names were also used. Interestingly, the First Nation that I am a member of, the Nisga'a, had not given the missionaries a name for Bigfoot in the local language. However, that did not mean the Nisga'a had no name for the creatures. It meant that they did not share those names with the missionaries. Perhaps they did not want to incur any bad luck by discussing it.

The Nisga'a have names, stories, legends, and a local dance referencing the Bigfoot. My mother told me that when she was a young girl visiting her grandparents in the Nisga'a village of Gitwinksihlkw (People of the Lizard), something tried to open the door handle late one evening. The adults seemed alarmed, and when my mother asked who it was, her grandfather replied, "it is the Hagwilok", (the Beast Man). While sightings in the Nass Valley are quite common nowadays, some of the Nisga'a people still whisper when they speak about it. As the legend goes, if you see a Bigfoot, you will either get very lucky in the near future or you will die. Also, if you manage to take a child away from a mother Bigfoot, and return her child to her, you will receive great luck. But do not turn away from her, as she will claw up your back.

Along with the legends, there are local stories of people in earlier generations who apparently managed to catch a Bigfoot child and return it to the mother. Those men went on to make a lot of money in the fishing industry. In contrast, a man who had turned his back on a female Bigfoot awoke on the ground with deep lacerations on his back. These stories may explain why Nisga'a informants to the missionaries had not divulged the Nisga'a terms for Bigfoot. In general, the terms Indigenous groups use are localized and are not a global representation. This is an important distinction because although I must assume that there are significant populations of these animals roaming North America, I have no firm footing to assume that they all belong to the same species of animal. Therefore, Bigfoot as a term for the species that live here in the Nass Valley works for me. Also, they have big feet, which I will discuss later and provide photos I have taken.

Along with occasionally discussing psychological-based theories, I will present several stories that have been relayed to me by members of the Nisga'a Nation, as well as non-Nisga'a people that have lived or visited the Nass Valley. More importantly, I will present my personal stories and place photos throughout the book relating to my experiences. Based on these first and second-hand testimonials, I will make an argument supporting the existence of Bigfoot, particularly about its existence in the Nass Valley. Moreover, I will speak about the existence of this species as if hundreds or thousands of people have seen it; as if thousands of tracks have been seen, photographed, and cast; as if the animals have been photographed and videotaped numerous times; as if DNA is suggestive that an unrecognized primate species live in North American forests. Hey, wait a minute! All of those things are true. This book is not intended to convince non-believers that Bigfoot exists. This book is intended to add to the conversation about Bigfoot and respecting the opinions of the different camps. As a Bigfoot researcher, I do not run around the forest at night (occasionally if my vehicle breaks down or gets stuck), knock on trees (Ok occasionally), or bellow to try and get a response (I have made different sounds when I hear them vocalizing around me but they never respond). However, later in the book, I will explain why I normally do not need to do these things. To whet your appetite, here is a tidbit. Three nights ago, an adolescent male Bigfoot was in the field behind my house, trying to mimic an owl. Later on, I will explain how I know that he is a he, how I know he is an adolescent, and how I know it wasn't an owl.

Psychology and personal experiences are a couple of ways to illu-minate the Bigfoot discussion. While I am not a conspiracy theorist, well, not about everything anyway, when I started doing research into Bigfoot, I did not believe there to be a government cover-up of the phenomena. Actually, up until eight years ago, when I started my PhD program, I thought that people who espoused a government cover-up of Bigfoot were conspiracy theorists. When I admitted to being guilty earlier for jumping to psychologically-based theoretical conclusions, this was one example: guilty for making assumptions, jumping to conclusions, and labeling. In psychology, we call these mental shortcuts or thinking distortions. Therefore, a third aspect of this book will be discussing the conspiracy theory, and I will present some Indigenous stories, internet accounts, and personal accounts that suggest this cover-up notion may have a basis in reality.

I will introduce the evidential content of this book by discussing the kinds of evidence that seem to be the most common. The first and most important source of information regarding Bigfoot is the numerous eye witness sightings. Based on eye witness sightings, especially those that last minutes or longer, Bigfoot has been known to travel in small family groups, larger extended family groups, and groups large enough to warrant being called "tribes" by early European settlers. Sightings indicate that there is a range of Bigfoot sizes, age groups, and sexes. Although eyewitnesses have reported a range of colors from white to black, studies of hair samples indicate that Bigfoot hair has a reddish tinge at a microscopic level. Bigfoot has been observed eating a variety of foods, including fish, plants and roots, rodents, ungulates (deer, moose, and goats), birds, and human food when available. Bigfoot has been reported to create sounds by hitting logs with sticks and banging rocks together. Bigfoot vocalizations have been reported, including grunting, bellowing, screaming, whistling, animal mimicry, and a form of talking. Although Bigfoot has been reported to walk upright, it has also been seen moving on all fours and crawling on its stomach. Although similar to humans, the foot is not identical to human feet; the weight is more in the front of the foot with a flatter overall presence; the front of the foot is more flexible than a human foot; and the big toe of the Bigfoot can move inward like a thumb according to some eye witness. The flexibility of the foot and toes may be a major reason why Bigfoot find rugged environments a suitable habitat.

The consistency of the historical record in written form by early European settlers, told orally and carved on totem poles in Aboriginal cultures, and more recently through oral, written, and photo-based technology in modern times, is credible evidence that the Bigfoot has co-existed with humans for some time. When one looks at evolutionary theory, it might be argued that subpopulations of the original creature may have evolved over the millennia, contributing to the interesting diversity of observations in Bigfoot sightings. Some suggest that Bigfoot is a species known as Australopithicus Blacki, a very large ape thought to have become extinct in Asia ten thousand years ago. The boldest notion of all is that Bigfoot may be a forerunner of modern human beings, with some suggesting that it is a form of Neandertal. Although I am not a supporter of this notion, if this is true, Bigfoot may be one of the most important creatures on this planet; a central hub of evolutionary activity and general hominid body style modified and giving rise to several evolutionary forebearers of humans.

Consistent with evolutionary theory and cultural development theories, there is strong evidence to suggest that culturally-based behavior in human beings is structured around the availability of resources. One example is human marriage practices. Polyandry, polygynandry, and monogamy are all marriage practices utilized by modern human beings, and the choice of marriage model is generally related to the availability of resources. In terms of the limited evidence of Bigfoot social behavior, and growing knowledge of primate and human behavior, some inferences about Bigfoot can be made. As is the norm with Bigfoot sightings, most sightings are of single animals or small groups, usually three or fewer, indicating that for foraging purposes, Bigfoot tend to travel in small groups. Given the apparent sparseness of accessible nutrients in most wilderness settings, particularly North American coniferous forests, coupled with the propensity for large body size, it would make sense that Bigfoot group size would generally be restricted by the availability of relatively local resources. Males and females would probably have to forage separately, and varying sizes of territories would be needed depending on resource availability.

As with human cultures, some environments are more advanta-geous for sustaining larger animal populations, and in the case of Bigfoot, this should be no different. Because larger groups should be advantageous for hominid species in general, it is a cultural trait that should be selected based on evolutionary theory if the environmental conditions are correct or if the creatures in question could manipu-late the environment to make the conditions better. Given the abun-dance of food resources, for example, near water sources, it would make some sense that larger populations of these creatures may have been sustained. As with human beings, illustrated by the Inuit people (larger brains and more robust capillary system), genetic changes to improve survival in environmentally challenging conditions can occur within a species. A variety of Bigfoot cultural and physical diversity would not only be possible given the variety of stable eco-systems it would be expected. For example, climatic conditions such as temperature may contribute to genetic differences in body size and hair patterns.

Although as a generalist, like modern humans, Bigfoot may have specialized to survive in several different environments, slowly shaping different genotypes and phenotypical representations. Bigfoot has been sighted in most environments within North America, including water (rivers, creeks, and lagoons), and has been noted to be at home in ocean waters, sometimes observed swimming miles off-shore. Bigfoot has been seen in mountainous environments and described as being very agile and moving with grace and strength in the most awkward of positions. Along with genotype and phenotype issues, Bigfoot may have adapted to different environments by changing its social structure, a technique modern human populations use. As Bigfoot settled in very productive areas, it makes sense that family groups would be more inclined to share territory, and a reduction of conflicts and group cooperation would eventually develop. Left long enough to develop, evolution would select those traits for the creature to better adapt to living in a more complex social network. The expected specialization of Bigfoot populations over time is consistent with the historical accounts of Bigfoot encounters. Bigfoot populations were noted in the historical record to behave more like modern humans than the typical modern Bigfoot encounter, including more day-time activity and living in larger groups. Early European settlers reported that Bigfoot lived in large groups, and the settlers sometimes referred to them as living in tribes. Bigfoot was reported as sometimes attacking settlers in a coordinated fashion using clubs as weapons, and in some cases, it was reported that settlers fought back, sometimes killing the animals. These reports indicate that some Bigfoot populations may have grown complex social systems interdependent on each other for survival. It also makes sense that these sub-populations would be the first to disappear as the result of competition with settlers or Indigenous Peoples.

Along with the written record, documented European settlers, Dr. John Bindernagel, and other researchers, have tried to make the point that Bigfoot creatures have been captured in numerous countries including Canada. Dr. Grover Krantz and John Green reported a story that allegedly occurred near Yale British Columbia, which an elder resident later verified. The Bigfoot adolescent known as "Jacko" was reported to have been captured and later taken on a train by a fellow working for a circus, where Jacko later died. The story was reported in the local paper and verified at the time by the participants involved in the capture. However, a descendent of one of the residents of Yale claimed that their relative (who would have known about the incident, according to the descendent) told him that the event never happened. If you search the internet, it has become one of the stories that "HAVE BEEN DEBUNKED" based on someone's account of what their uncle's brother's late father-in-law said didn't happen. Apparently, debunking has become pretty easy these days. It is often disguised in the form of taking an investigative reporter approach, comprised of research filled with evidentiary holes, a statement suggesting the author is the final arbiter, and a conclusion usually relayed with arrogance and a supposition that their process of "objective" investigation has somehow elevated their opinion, superseding the opinions of others.

In addition to eyewitness sightings, other compelling sources of evidence warrant at least having an open mind about the existence of Bigfoot. There have been several footprints found and casts made that support the existence of an unknown upright walking creature in North America. Although one must agree that footprints are easy to hoax, and several hoaxes have been uncovered and admitted to, there is no logical conclusion that all track discoveries are hoaxes. In fact, one of the tracks that we found was fresh, created within a few minutes of us finding it, and left by a foul-smelling creature that was extremely heavy. Some people have argued that the discovery of tracks of any other animal would be accepted at face value, however, when it comes to Bigfoot, tracks do not meet the threshold of acceptability. With Bigfoot tracks, the evidence bar has been raised. The raising of the bar has occurred even though tracks have been found in extremely remote places and that more than one person has discovered them. In addition, identical tracks have been found over time and space, and extreme detail such as lines on the foot-prints known as dermal ridges and physical developmental anomalies would be near impossible to hoax. Furthermore, varied-size prints, deep depressions indicating great weight, and long stride marks suggest that people would have difficulty replicating most of these elements. Still, we have trouble accepting this evidence. Although tracks can be hoaxed, and mistakes can easily be made, footprint analysis is an accepted form of forensic science.

Photographs and video-recordings are evidence that has not met the Skeptic threshold and moreover, have been the brunt of much ridicule. The problem with photograph and video recordings is the quality is usually poor, or images are taken from a significant distance. Even with the Patterson video, controversy has followed. My trail-cam video of several Bigfoot is no different. I will explain my video-recording in a later chapter and present the still photos of the recording. In the Patterson video, however, several things suggest the video is capturing a Bigfoot. First, the creature seems large, and its frame and gait indicate a heavy set, strong creature. When the creature turns to look at the camera, one can see two breasts swinging into view in a very natural state of motion. I find it hard to believe that before the days that Hollywood's greatest costume designers created such a poor facsimile of primates in Planet of the Apes, such a realistic-looking creature could be reproduced at that time. Although some have claimed that they knew people who have participated in the hoax, the main players have never publicly proclaimed that they partook in a hoax. More recently, the Patterson video clip has undergone extensive computer analysis, in which facial and other muscles were concluded to be natural. One analysis even showed a hernia bulging with every step. If indeed it was a hoax, and this is a perspective that any balanced-thinking person must contemplate, it was truly an excellent job.

Another video recording was taken by two individuals of a creature lying on the forest floor, trying to hide behind a log. Upon close analysis of the footage, one can make out a foot exposing five curled toes, toenails and all. The length and shape of the body indicated that it was human-like, and the intermittent view of the inquisitive face peeking under the fallen log suggested both fear and curiosity. The two men at the time were gagging due to the smell of the creature.

One of my favorite videos can be found on the internet. It is of a male primate walking on a trail and stopping to look up at a trail-cam in a tree. By the look on his face, he is not impressed. There are a couple of interesting aspects to the video. First, the creature has one damaged eye or may have only had one eye. This is of personal significance, which I will discuss in a later chapter. Second, after carefully looking at the video several times, I noticed something moving, but I couldn't clearly see it. I got a hold of a high-definition computer and could see what was moving. Adult Content Warning: After glaring at the camera, the Bigfoot sets his weight on his back foot and moves forward with a bit of a swaying motion. When he does, one can make out his erect penis and swaying testicles. What is interesting about this is that his penis resembled that of a chimpanzee (I took a primatology course in university). However, his testicles resembled those of a human. All three types of known chimpanzees have large testicles, but this creature did not. If it was a hoax, it was well-thought-out. However, most photographs and videos are of poor quality, based on poor focus, hurried shots, and poor lighting and obstructions. In addition, hoaxed pictures are easy to manufacture and, with some creativity, can be quite convincing. Recently, a Bigfoot researcher produced an extremely clear video of two different Bigfoot. However, after some technically savvy folks carefully analyzed the video using computer technology, they declared it a hoax and presented a convincing argument as to why. My own analysis of the videos (I am not a video analysis expert) resulted in the same conclusion because two separate creatures were video-recorded standing behind the same branch. Therefore, although videotapes and photographs can be interesting topics for conversation, one must be cautious when making conclusions based on them.

If eyewitness testimony (To Skeptics, please don't refer to Elizabeth Loftus's research), footprints, videotape, and photographs do not meet the Skeptic threshold, what will suffice? Although a balanced perspective might agree that the collective evidence thus far is sufficient to warrant a second look, the evidence is not conclusive. The key to proving the existence of any creature is the same key to proving the existence of Bigfoot: scientific evidence so strong that it is logically irrefutable. In the past few decades, advances in DNA technology have made possible the ability to prove the existence of this species. This premise, which is now a part of our collective consciousness, is that every organism possesses a DNA makeup that is unique to itself. In addition, the premise relies on the findings that similar species of animals have similar genetic make-ups and can even be measured as to statistical similarity between DNA. Along with accepting the scientific validity of the DNA model, we also rest our premise on the understanding that people at this time do not possess the technology to artificially create DNA, although we do have the ability to construct existing DNA into new forms.

Numerous samples of alleged Bigfoot hair have been brought forth by different people. Some of these samples have been examined and identified as belonging to known animals. Other hair samples supposedly yielded DNA that did not match either human or any known primate species but seemed to have characteristics consistent with a primate. Based on what we collectively accept about DNA technology, one must accept that a creature not yet cataloged by science provided the hair from which the DNA was extracted. One can reasonably accept that the other sources of evidence are inconclusive. However, a balanced perspective must accept the findings of the DNA evidence. The reality however is that DNA evidence is not well documented, and experts have soundly criticized a recent journal article regarding Bigfoot DNA.

Again, it may be difficult for you to accept the reality of Bigfoot, and I, in a similar position, would likely agree. However, I have seen individual Bigfoot creatures on seven occasions and, therefore, I know they exist. As a result, I write this book from the perspective that Bigfoot does exist and will begin by shedding some light on why others find it so difficult to accept. Occams Razor is a story taught in psychology that guides a perspective that says that the simplest solution to explain something contains the fewest assumptions. So, when people say they saw a hairy upright walking primate, is the simplest solution that they were on drugs, misidentifying an upright walking bear with human-like arms, hands, and face? Or is the simplest solution that they saw a hairy upright walking primate? In the next chapter, I will elaborate on ontology, or the nature of reality, and epistemology, or how we gather knowledge in relation to the Bigfoot phenomena.

2

WHY AND WHAT TO BELIEVE IN

B efore we start to search out the elusive creature, I think we must build a framework for understanding the Bigfoot phenomenon. Without a framework, stretching our mental representation of reality regarding Bigfoot can distract the most disciplined of thinkers. Indigenous worldviews incorporate Bigfoot as a real creature. It is a part of their cultural view of reality (ontology). While Indigenous cultures base their beliefs on empirical experience, Bigfoot is some-times also a part of their spiritual belief system. For example, some Nisga'a people believe Bigfoot to be a Naxnok (a spiritual being who is also a shape-shifter). I want to be clear that a cultural worldview does not mean that everyone in the culture views reality through that lens.

I have done informal surveys with Nisga'a people. Approximately one in twenty have seen a Bigfoot or thought they had some type of experience with one. Fifty percent, however, knew someone who claimed to have seen a Bigfoot. Some Nisga'a believe in the existence of Bigfoot, and some do not. However, the ontology of the Western worldview is that Bigfoot does not exist. Again, many non-Indigenous people believe in the existence of Bigfoot, but from a collective Western cultural perspective, Bigfoot does not exist. Therefore, we have a divergence between worldviews. The Indigenous cultural worldview is not going to be swayed that Bigfoot does not exist. In fact, proving a negative or proving that something does not exist is impossible. Therefore, to reach a collective agreement that Bigfoot does exist, it needs to be determined based on available scientific evidence, which, if found credible, can be incorporated into our collective consciousness. Accepting evidence as fact by the greater society will allow the research community to systematically study the Bigfoot phenomenon. In order to properly study Bigfoot, numerous evidence-gathering tools and, more importantly, committed people who are willing to spend years in the field will be required.

Given the financial and human resources needed to properly study Bigfoot, a secure relationship with the mainstream scientific community is necessary. Oho! He has brought up the issue of science, you say. Yes, victoriously cries the Skeptic, I have him now. For the Skeptic understands that his/her brand of philosophy and psychology can spin such a web of interesting tangents as to stifle even the heartiest of believers. I, and the camp that accompanies me, also raised our arms in victory, assured that our point of view would inevitably be vindicated, and therefore, it was correct. But we need to acknowledge that the skeptical position is not wrong. Cognitive psychology tells us that one 'should' be thinking and behaving exactly as they are, based on their experiential history and particularly how their beliefs have been culturally shaped. To expect them to think and behave differently, and by extension, for us to be distressed when those expectations are not realized, simply makes no sense. In simple terms, this means that the level of evidence required to convince a Skeptic or change the mind of a believer means meeting different thresholds. When the issue is understood as meeting the differing thresholds of people, differing value-laden positions can be understood. However, the correctness issue remains and continues to be blurred depending on the individual.

First, we must agree that a person's perspective can only be based on their experience of things. These experiences can come from external sources (sensation and perception) and internal sources (thinking). In addition, external and internal information has been said to come from a type of cosmic information source. This cosmic source of information is relevant to Indigenous cultures through Shamans or the like and psychics in Western cultures. Therefore, when a person comes into contact with information that another person has not come into contact with, that person will view things differently if they are convinced that the evidence is accurate. As a result, a person's perspective is the sum of, and then some, the experiences in their lives up to that point in time. Therefore, if we knew all of the predictors that comprised human thoughts and behaviors, and we do know many of them, theoretically, we could, with good accuracy, predict human beliefs and behavior. For example, in a landmark study of couples and divorce, Dr. John Gottman and associates discovered several predictors that predicted the probability of divorce among their study subjects at an astonishing 94%. However, although we are getting better at understanding factors in human behavior, we are far from being able to accurately predict human thought and behavior in complex situations.

The point of suggesting that thoughts and behaviors are somewhat predictable is to make the point that thoughts and behaviors result from a subjective reality based on a person's experiential history. Therefore, we can agree that a person's point of view 'should' be that way based on their reality, and furthermore, that no one individual can claim that their reality has more inherent worth or value than the reality of another individual in the absence of a collectively agreed upon fact. If this is the case, then we must agree that our points of reality are somehow cognitively equal. If our history validates our differing views, and yet are somehow still equal, then changing our views will not result in them being any more or less equal but simply in agreement with each other due to some shared experience. The point of all of this is to suggest that one person's thoughts and behaviors 'should' be just as they are and to suggest that they should not be suggests missing both the components of experiential history and the equality of different experiential-based realities.

Accepting the point of view of others does not mean that we have to agree with them. We disagree because we believe that we have access to information that suggests that our point of view is more correct, and someone who does not agree believes that he has access to information that makes him/her think they are correct. The interesting notion is that the reference point is the same in that the crossroads is where one agrees that certain specific evidence becomes information or fact. The believers in Bigfoot suggest that evidence they have been exposed to, or that they have experienced is enough for them to accept Bigfoot as real. The Skeptics have several ways of addressing their own perspective. However, their position is more difficult because it is based on attempting to prove a negative, which logic dictates is impossible. In addition, the Skeptic must resort to suggestions of psychological models that explain such mis-perceptions. However, this is the weakest evidence, and the notion that replicating a simple perceptual phenomenon in a laboratory can explain real-life experience makes little practical sense.

Don't get me wrong, I see the importance of skeptic-orientated people and the balance they bring to the discussion. Often, the skeptical role is the appropriate one and can simply be a form of critical thinking surrounding any issue. Skeptics also get a bum rap label, and again, this may be unwarranted. Most Skeptics are regular people with a pretty well-balanced opinion of issues. In general, Skeptics are intelligent, and that makes sense because to develop such a complex and compelling argument against the existence of Bigfoot, a tremendous amount of intelligence must be at play. I myself am skeptical-orientated, and even though my experiences indicate that other concepts exist in reality, I don't have to accept that every claim of a similar experience from someone else has merit. However, concerning skepticism, it needs to be pointed out that the skeptical position has been shown to be incorrect in the past. In a paradoxical sense, the dance of positions can diverge: A Skeptic suggesting that the foundation of past fallacies not be distorted to influence their current position being entertained, and the Bigfoot believers suggesting their evidence not be distorted to influence their current position being entertained. Please, let me go on to entertain you.

The main problem is when the human position distorts the facts, becoming dogmatic on any particular issue. When this happens, the evidence sufficient to convince such a person grows in proportion to the magnitude of the "discovery" of the creature itself. Cognitive defense systems come to the aid of the cerebrally-orientated Skeptic, who use them to protect their own version of realty and allow them to claim that their position is correct. However, entrenched in their dogmatic approach, Skeptics are society's self-declared watchdogs of hoaxes, and more media coverage is required to advertise the necessity and usefulness of their role in balancing public discourse. Skeptics and the holy order of thinking they espouse, known as the scientific method, keep us on our toes. Moreover, Skeptics have shown that many claims of the supernatural were financially motivated, and supernatural phenomena were replicable as hoaxes. However, this does not mean that every undiscovered phenomenon that can be somehow accounted for was actually accounted for.

Although replication is generally seen as an important step in scientific inquiry to transform information into knowledge, replication of something in a laboratory setting and generalizing it to real-life situations does not ensure that the original phenomenon was the same as the replicated one. Two separate phenomena can produce similar perceptions in people because we lack the sensory systems to distinguish between finer differences in physical stimuli. For example, an illusion to replicate a phenomenon may involve reproducing a light source, and we would be unable to discriminate between the physical properties of the light. Even when some aspect of a phenomenon can be reproduced in a laboratory, it is a stretch to conclude that these findings can explain rare and complex human experiences. I believe that at some point in the future, it will be inevitable that a Bigfoot body or other form of irrefutable evidence will be discovered, and the notion of laboratory explanations will be revealed for its fallacy of thought. In recent years, several researchers decided to replicate a number of influential psychology studies.

Unfortunately, they were only able to replicate just under half of them.

If the question is about evidence, then we must agree on what acceptable methods of knowledge gathering lead to what a culture deems as acceptable evidence (epistemology), or how we know what is real. Indigenous cultures more readily accept eyewitness accounts of strange phenomena than Western culture. However, even when evidence such as tracks is acceptable from a Western standpoint concerning one type of animal, in the case of Bigfoot, tracks are not acceptable as evidence. Sure, someone can construct big feet and make tracks. However, would this necessarily have to explain every incident of finding large human-like footprints? Right now, you are probably thinking, "what does this have to do with believing in Bigfoot you longwinded #$%@#?" It means that information is processed through a cognitive defense system that basically censors incoming data. In psychological terms, we can accommodate new information by accepting it and modifying our belief system to change our perspective, or we can assimilate it by incorporating it into our existing schema and not changing our perspective. Basically, this means is that we can look at the same data, come to different conclusions, and it is all perfectly legitimate; the evidence does not have to be accurate, only that one believes it is or not. This statement goes both ways in processing information, and the spoken and unspoken rules or heuristics people use to judge information. It is like casting a net with small holes versus a net with large holes. If the evidence is weak, someone with a net with small holes will catch it, even though it may be likely that some of the evidence does not represent the validity of a phenomenon. If a person has a net with large holes, it will miss most of the evidence. However, some of the evidence disregarded might be valid. This is the cultural dilemma of what sources of information constitute knowledge. Sometimes we can fudge by not disregarding it outright but redirecting the informa-tion into the "Ok I'm not sure" file. However, it still does not allow people with different cultural worldviews to collectively accept the information as knowledge in a multi-cultural context.

We are all hoping that there is some uniform reference point at which we could ascribe some sense of worth to our position, and maybe the only way to do this is to suggest that, in the case of Bigfoot, the creature exists or not. The Skeptic suggests that evidence has not been presented that would support the creature's existence, and the believer agrees that this threshold was met long ago. I have argued that both perspectives are equally valid, although one is right and one is wrong based on the reference point of whether Bigfoot exists or not. The job now is to try and convince Skeptics that the evidence for Bigfoot is actually a basis for knowledge, and life can go one with a renewed passion for the pursuit of a more conventional and multicultural approach to knowledge gathering.

Well, it is, of course, easy for me to be skeptical about most claims of strange things, and just as easy for me to claim that Bigfoot exists because of my several experiences. I am sort of caught in between cultural worldviews, that of Indigenous Peoples, and that of Western society. This may seem inconsistent with each other, but it is about my experiential history in both areas. My psychological training and tendency to use scientific explanations for previously unsolved problems suggest that I follow this general scientific route to accept data as knowledge. On the other side, I have experienced several interactions with Bigfoot, and in my mind, I am correct in claiming that Bigfoot is real in a reality with a reference point that we can all agree on. Being the author of this book, and that my experiences have convinced me of the existence of Bigfoot, my take on this issue will, of course, be biased. As I "know" that Bigfoot exists, I also know that the position of the Skeptic cannot be correct if their position is that Bigfoot does not exist. However, it seems unjust to assume that they have not looked at the same evidence as me, and therefore, something else must be influencing their thoughts. And no, they cannot hide behind scientific principles because scientific evidence has supported the existence of Bigfoot. Human beings are multi-level creatures, designed for both independent and inter-dependent thought. Numerous biological, social, and environmental systems strongly influence our thoughts and behaviors. To understand Skeptics is to understand ourselves because we are skeptical towards and believers in all types of phenomena.

The hormone testosterone is one example of how biological processes may impact our thinking patterns. In some labs, special mice that cannot produce testosterone are created. When injected with testosterone, they immediately change their social behavior and begin to exhibit aggressive mating and territorial behavior. Although humans are largely unaware that hormones are associated with their thoughts and behavior, a biological process occurs between hormones and thoughts. In psychology, a theory known as the two-factor theory shows how when people are psychologically aroused for a physical reason, such as adrenaline in their system, they associate the cause of that feeling with something or someone around them. Because they make the attribution that their physiological arousal is caused by an incorrect source, their behavior becomes consistent with that incorrect source rather than the actual source. This misattribution is theorized to be a major cause of relationship problems. These biological influences on our thinking processes are not to be underestimated, as they work in concert at a social level. At a basic level, many theorists suggest that fear is a primal emotion of man, and it is this emotion that skeptical arguments sometimes pander to. Sigmund Freud was one of the first people to identify the role of fear in the unconscious and how fear influences thinking and behavior. In terms of thinking, strategies such as denial, projection, and rationalization are used by people to avoid bringing threatening unconscious thoughts into awareness. This, however, can result in consequences such as psychological disorders resulting from burying traumatic experiences. Freud's theories are important to my position because I believe that Skeptics resort to denial and then rationalization, a classic pair in Freudian psychology.

From a behavioral psychology perspective, I argue that Skeptics have formed their beliefs due to some form of behavior and reward process, often referred to as learning theory. Behavioral psychology suggests that thoughts and feelings are simply points that compel humans to seek out rewarding, pleasurable sensations and avoid displeasing ones. It makes sense if you look at it from a social learning perspective. Scientists who go out on the edge to investigate phenomena not considered acceptable by mainstream science have long faced the prospect of professional ridicule, a form of punishment. The thought of facing ridicule from your peers must be a very fearful thought. The ridicule and possible ostracization from the scientific community could also lead to financial difficulties and jeopardizing one's career. Just ask Charles Darwin. The mainstream science community ridiculed Darwin's theory of evolution for many years. From a social learning perspective, scientists who accept evidence outside of the scientific method are going against the grain and are putting themselves at risk. A simple way of looking at how thinking patterns are influenced by learning principles can be illustrated with the cognitive/behavioral anger model. Anger can be understood as being functional because it gives the person short-term control over a situation. This short-term control can be very rewarding, and as the theory of the Law of Effect goes, similar behavior will be more likely in the future. With some chronically angry people, it has been found that they are chronically in a state of physiological arousal and that anger behavior has been rewarded in the past.

Therefore, from a strict behavioral perspective, the thoughts and feelings which have preceded anger are largely immaterial. This is because the anger behavior is predictable based on the person's punishment and reward history. When the thoughts and feelings of people have been researched, it was not a surprise to find out that many chronically angry people use the same thinking and feeling strategies that contribute to anger and anger-related behavior. Anger has been shown to have three main components: that a person thinks that they have been harmed, that the harm was done on purpose, and that inflicting harm on them was wrong, or that the harm "shouldn't" have happened. At least ten thinking errors have been associated with converting physiological arousal into anger. A quick list of the thinking mistakes sometimes referred to as cognitive errors are: Jumping to conclusions; All or none thinking; Mental filter; Minimizing and maximizing; Emotional reasoning; Disqualifying the positive; Shoulding; Labeling; Overgeneralizing; and Personalization. When these thinking mistakes are explored with individuals with anger problems, it becomes apparent that the three components of anger are almost always constructed with most of the thinking mistakes.

These thinking errors, however, do not only contribute to anger. They also contribute to the beliefs of normal emotionally-regulated people, such as us and Skeptics. Albert Ellis, the father of modern cognitive psychology, suggested that any position on an issue that is strongly espoused or stated dogmatically often includes the use of thinking errors. He included fanatics and Skeptics in this group. Given that the Skeptic position is largely based on disconfirmation of evidence, the room for error is immense. Remember the analogy of a net having large or small holes. A Skeptic has a net with very large holes, a belief system in which little or no evidence will get caught. As I believe that evidence of Bigfoot that would get caught in most nets exists, I suggest that the large holed net of the Skeptic is supported by the ten thinking errors. The mental filter is one of the obvious thinking errors committed by the Skeptic. This thinking strategy is necessary to keep out all unwanted information threatening to the Skeptic's position. Using a pessimistic attitude towards the phenomenon, incoming information is filtered and perceived at a conscious level as being unimportant. In addition, a mental filter supports using other cognitive thinking errors. For example, Skeptics jump to conclusions when it comes to Bigfoot information. The first conclusion they jump to is that the evidence must be a hoax. Indeed, there have been hoaxes, and some have been very amusing. However, the suggestion that all evidence must be a hoax because similar evidence had been hoaxed in the past, simply makes the net holes too large to catch any evidence. Another example is that Skeptics suggest that eyewitness sightings are misperceptions. Again, cases citing perceptual illusions, mass hysteria, and the eyewitness work of researchers like Elizabeth Loftus is a stretch to explain complex human experiences such as visual, auditory, and olfactory perceptions in a real-world environment.

Skeptics also use another thinking distortion, sometimes known as black and white thinking. This thinking illustrates the position of the Skeptic that they will only believe the existence of Bigfoot when they see a Bigfoot or one is captured or found dead. With such a position, one can see why the Skeptic does not accept any alternative evidence that Bigfoot exists. The Skeptic has created a net with holes so large that it can only catch one piece of evidence: A Bigfoot. The Skeptic is also a master of minimizing and maximizing information so as to maintain their evidence net. Minimizing refers to minimizing the importance of certain information, such as sloughing off eyewitness sightings as bear sightings. Maximizing is the other side of the coin and refers to maximizing certain theories to challenge Bigfoot accounts. One example of maximizing is laboratory experiments in which perceptions can be manipulated, which Skeptics suggest accounts for misperceptions when people encounter a Bigfoot. A related thinking distortion is disqualifying the positive. Disqualified positives include individual experiences as well as cumulative experiences. The evidence for the existence of Bigfoot is based on personal experiences, group experiences, and longitudinal or cumulative evidence over time. What makes this thinking distortion so insidious is that it disqualifies the collective human experience in order to satisfy a cultural principle of epistemology. Even when evidence is consistent with that epistemology, it is still disqualified as not being good enough.

The Skeptic also uses the thinking distortion of "shoulding." Albert Ellis described the word 'should' as one in which we 'should on ourselves' when we use it. One of the Skeptic's famous 'shoulding' lines is that if Bigfoot has been around for so long, we 'should' have found a body or bones by now. This is, of course, a fallacy of thought. It may be true (I'm not sure) that a body or bones have not been found. However, on what grounds can an argument be correct that we should have found a body or bones? A Skeptic must be reminded that bodies and bones in the wild are usually spread over vast distances and consumed by animals. I am an avid mushroom picker, and I agree with the argument that the bones of certain animals are hard to come by. The wolves in our area contribute to carcasses being found. However, I have only found a bear carcass once, and it had been killed by poachers high in the mountains. In the 40 years of being an outdoors person, I have only come across one bear skull. However, I would argue that if every inch of every forest and mountain was explored over a long period of time, then it might be sensible to say that we 'should' have found some bones or other physical evidence proving that Bigfoot exists. That is, unless Bigfoot bury their dead or dispose of them in some way that would make them hard to locate. We have no idea. Until we scour every inch above and below the ground, I guess we will have to accept that maybe, at this point in time, we should not have been able to find that particular evidence.

One of the Skeptics' most interesting thinking errors is one that we all use every day: the art of labeling. Kooks and hoaxers are a couple of examples. Labeling is related to over-generalizing. Some people are hoaxers; therefore, all evidence of Bigfoot has been placed by hoaxers. The final thinking error on my list is that Skeptics sometimes personalize a controversial issue and can become emotionally entrenched in their position. It is very difficult for people to see the value in another's position when they are closed off emotionally. I believe that if the Skeptic could realize that the believer's position is independent of the Skeptic position, the defense system of the Skeptic could be relaxed, and perhaps they would be more open to shrinking the holes in their evidence net.

In addition to thinking errors, several thinking strategies are detrimental to people coming to a more balanced conclusion. People first learn about concepts slowly, building up their experience based on common examples of a concept, such as chairs and stools as pieces of furniture that you sit on. These concepts can be applied to deductive thinking, in which a new item can be added to an existing schema. The issue is whether the premises are correct; if so, the following conclusion will be logically correct. One example is; only birds have feathers; a parrot has feathers; then a parrot must be a bird. The conclusion will be true as long as the first two premises are true. Unfortunately, we take cognitive shortcuts as we grow and our experiences become more varied. While important to efficient thinking, shortcuts also result in more errors when applying deductive thinking. There are several known cognitive biases that support our personal beliefs. However, they are easily exposed as shortcut errors upon analysis.

One of the influences on the decision-making process of people is the concept of stereotyped threat. It refers to the impact on people's decision-making process and performance based on a perceived stereotype regarding that particular topic. An illustration of this can be described in terms of the stereotype that men are better than women at math. When placed in a room doing difficult math questions, women performed much worse than men. Another group of men and women were tested, but they were first told that the questions could not distinguish gender. For this group, there were no differences in performance! Psychology practitioners know first-hand the layers that can influence an individual's thinking; some to the point of pathology. Others, such as cognitive biases, are rather normal but can still be dangerous. Canada stayed out of the Iraq war because our leaders interpreted the evidence differently than the leaders of other countries, but they had access to the same evidence. As powerful as these influences are by themselves on our thought patterns, when we use them in conjunction with each other, they can support a large holed net where virtually no evidence or data will get caught, limiting our ability to transform information into knowledge. Then, out come the measuring scales, and together, we will explore the physical reality of evidence regarding the Bigfoot. We must explore physical reality because it is the only objective measure, but we can also explore more subjective views on the subject. We will proceed onto my favorite parts of this book; relaying the stories of others and telling my own stories about the misty giants of the lava beds.

3

WII XLAAKWSGUM GAT

The Nass Valley is a remarkable place. It is home to Canada's most recent volcano, and the dynamic landscape of the lava beds stretches for miles. Past earthly rumbles are echoed in the memory of the jagged peaks of moss and lichen-covered lava rock. The Nass Valley has a wide diversity of plant and animal life, ecosystems, and microclimates. For me, it is a sacred place that will truly take one's breath away. Sometimes, when the sun rays shine through openings in the clouds and onto the lava beds, one is reminded of magical places and a time before people. The Nass Valley is the setting for this book, and although sightings have been common around most of the Nass Valley, this book deals largely with sightings localized around specific areas. The localization of sightings is an important issue for several reasons. The first is that sightings around specific areas indicate Bigfoot territories or travel routes used by Bigfoot. In addition, these concentrated sightings and experiences might shed some light on Bigfoot's behavior and family structure. More often than not, sightings in the Nass Valley have been experienced by multiple witnesses. This observation lends credibility to the existence of Bigfoot. Another important reason for localized sightings is the convergence of historical sightings in the same area. Perhaps the most important reason relating to localized sightings is the potential for strategic research. In the past, people who researched Bigfoot tended to focus on recent sighting and then attempted to search the local area. The information gathered was haphazard at best and there was no clear strategy for gathering information, and no guiding principles that could be reproduced by others searching for the same evidence. Localized sightings over time allow for observation of behavior patterns, and proper research might be conducted from these patterns. To set a geographical context for this book, I will introduce the four Nisga'a communities in the Nass Valley.

Gingolx (Kincolith):

The community of Gingolx, or the Place of the Skulls, is the newest to be established of the Nisga'a communities. It is situated at the mouth of the Nass River where it meets the Pacific Ocean and is touted as the Seafood Capital of the Nass. Until about 15 years ago, access to Gingolx was limited to private boats, a ferry service, and seaplane flights. After negotiating the Nisga'a Treaty, a highway was built through the Nass Valley, linking all four Nisga'a villages. The people of Gingolx have their share of Bigfoot stories. On an initial internet search, I found a story of a local resident who had watched a Bigfoot fishing while swimming in a local creek for approximately ten minutes. When I started flying into Gingolx to work as a psychotherapist, I immediately started documenting some of their stories.

One of the local grocery store owners in the community was very interested in my Bigfoot story (at that time, I only had one). He was very cynical of the people who did not believe in Bigfoot, as he had thought that he had heard the animal vocalizing on several occasions. As several other people in the community had told me of the same vocalizations that they had heard within the past few weeks, I was curious to listen to his story. As he leaned over the wooden railing at the top of the stairs leading to his store, he looked down at me and said, "I heard it, you know." "I heard it over the last few weeks." I was interested in the sound of the vocalizations because most of the people I had spoken to said it was a howling sound and that it was coming from very close to the village. Most of the people who had told me about it said that it was definitely not a person, that it was very loud, and that they had never heard it before. The grocery store owner also indicated that it was like a howling sound and that he had heard it around 3:00 am. Although he was quite impressed with how loud the vocalizations were, he was alarmed at the same time.

Earlier that week, the store owner was visiting a friend and had told him the story of the late-night howling. The friend asked him to wait while he looked for something on the internet. He called the grocery store owner over and asked if the sounds he heard were similar to the recordings another person made of a suspected Bigfoot and uploaded onto the internet. In describing this portion of the story, the store owner became somewhat emotional as he stated that the sounds that he heard on the internet recording were the same as the sounds he heard that night. I ran into the store owner several years later. He made a note to call me over and tell me about a recent encounter that his wife had. He said that his wife wanted to have a cigarette and went to the bedroom and opened the window to blow the smoke outside. It was early into the winter season, and there was some snow on the ground. When his wife opened the window, she came face to face with a Bigfoot that was looking in the window. His wife screamed, and some of the neighbors immediately came over to see if someone needed help. What was amazing about this story was that a set of tracks in the snow could be seen leading to the house. However, only two tracks could be seen leading away from the house. He said the tracks disappeared, which fueled his belief that Bigfoot were some kind of spiritual creature. To me, at that time, his story seemed incredulous. However, it was believable that his wife had come face to face with a Bigfoot looking in the window, but maybe not with the track interpretation. Also, other community members later told me of this incident. What I found incredulous was that only two tracks were found facing away from the house. Since I had already seen one Bigfoot by this time and had gone from non-believer to believer, I simply assumed that Bigfoot existed and they were a real living animal just like the rest of us. I must admit that it wasn't long after I saw my first Bigfoot and started talking to others about it that I became schooled in local cultural perspectives on Bigfoot, including that it may be a spiritual being called a Naxnok, possessing the ability to shapeshift, and even to disappear. Well, the truth is that I didn't buy that then, but later in this book, I will describe some amazing things that I have witnessed, but I do not attribute them to spiritual sources. So, what was my conclusion about the store owner's story? I entertained a few. The Bigfoot walked backward in the first row of footprints; the Bigfoot jumped onto the roof of the house and kept out of sight as the neighbors milled around the house; the Bigfoot jumped into a tree and swung from tree to tree until he got out of there; or there never was a Bigfoot, and he made up the whole thing. Since I could not understand how tracks could disappear in the snow, I resorted to some fantastical rationalized thinking. My thought process was normal: to try to explain some strange occurrence with mental gymnastics. My learning process about the Bigfoot phenomenon has certainly evolved over time. Some of my experiences in the past several years have caught up to what had previously been articulated by other people and cultures. Later in the book, I describe some weird things that I witnessed that may provide insight into this seemingly impossible scenario of only two footprints leading away from the home.

About four years ago, someone sent me a picture of a Bigfoot that they had taken near the Gingolx cemetery. The Bigfoot was standing partially behind a tree but looking directly at the person taking the picture. It was not a greatly muscled specimen, appeared to be a male, and it looked somewhat old. Its head was not round but had kind of an oblong shape to it. It had had high cheekbones, and its eyes were sunken in. There was no reflection from the eyes. It was difficult to tell what color it was because the picture was taken during the early evening hours, but it looked to have a uniform length of hair on its body, but you could only see the side of its body and its face. An interesting note about this picture was its face, but I will explain its significance later.

Two years ago, I was talking to a friend who had met a tourist who was sport fishing on the Nass River a couple of days earlier. He told my friend that as he was fishing, he heard a splashing sound around a bend in the shoreline. Thinking it may have been a bear, he walked over and peeked around the bend. It was not a bear but a Bigfoot up to his waist in water. The Bigfoot was watching the water, thrusting his hand into it and catching salmon. According to the tourist, the Bigfoot had caught a salmon with each hand and was hungrily eating the salmon, taking turns on each fish. The tourist slowly backtracked to where he was out of sight and climbed the bank to the road. He drove to Gingolx, met my friend, and asked him about the creature. My friend told him it was a Bigfoot and that the tourist should tell someone who works at the village government. The tourist took his advice and told someone at the village government. My friend ran into him later that day and asked him how his meeting went. He told my friend that the guy at the village government told him to go home and not to come back for a year. Well, I started laughing, and every Nisga'a I told that story to had a good chuckle. The reason it was humorous to us is because the advice that was given was cultural advice. By leaving immediately, no harm or bad luck would come to the tourist. After one year, the tourist would no longer have been exposed to the potential of harm or bad luck by seeing a Bigfoot.

Before the highway was extended to Gingolx, people from the upriver Nisga'a communities had to travel by boat down the river to Gingolx to visit and attend feasts. When I worked as a psychotherapist in the Nass, I would travel to Gingolx mostly by seaplane, but several times I traveled by boat. The Nisga'a people named many places along the river, and there was an outcrop along the river where the sea-grass grew. That flat section of ground was above the water line when the tide was out. I was talking to a younger fellow who told me that he and his dad were traveling past that section of the river, and at one end of the flats stood a Bigfoot. He said the Bigfoot was not looking at them but seemed preoccupied with something at the other end of the sea-grass flats. As they passed the other end, they could see a grizzly bear, and it appeared preoccupied with something in the direction of the Bigfoot. He told me that the bear stood up on its hind legs, sniffed the air, and immediately took off running into the forest. The two men looked back, and the Bigfoot had tilted his head back and appeared to be sniffing the air, and it turned around and quickly moved off into the forest.

One of the most interesting stories from around Gingolx came from two logging truck drivers travelling back to back. Along the stretch of highway between Gingolx and Laxgalts'ap, a section runs alongside the Nass River but is more like a fiord. The banks opposite the highway are very steep in some sections, and others are less steep. At one of the less step sections but about twenty feet off the highway, the two truck drivers saw two male Bigfoot beating each other. According to someone who spoke to one of the truck drivers, the hair was flying, and the encounter between the Bigfoot was very violent. The second truck driver got on his radio and asked if Bigfoot lived around there because he just saw two Bigfoot fighting on the side of the highway. Back in those days, there were few phones in the community, and most people communicated through VHF radios, which they kept on all the time for emergencies. A local woman picked up her VHF without missing a beat and said, "Are you sure they were fighting?" This brought a great deal of laughter within the community who had their VHF's on. Well, the Nisga'a people are quite humorous, which we pride ourselves on, and although the event was intensely relayed by one of the truck drivers, most people remember this event because of the humorous reply from the local woman.

The stretch of highway from Gingolx to Laxgalts'ap has had numerous sightings of Bigfoot. A number of sightings reported to me were around an area called Fishery Bay. It is an area where the Nisga'a harvest a member of the smelt family called oolichan. The oolichan is the first food available to Nisga'a in the new year. The Nisga'a people have another word for the oolichan, which translates to the savior fish, as it staved off starvation in times when the previous year was not so bountiful. Actually, the Nisga'a new year, called Hoobiyay, is in February, and the Nisga'a determine from the shape of the moon at that time of year whether the upcoming seasons will be bountiful. If the moon is shaped like a spoon or hoobix, the upcoming year will provide our people a wealth of bountiful resources. It may not be surprising that the Nisga'a named many of their months after food resources. March is named X̱saak, or "eating oolichans." The first feed of oolichans is an important ceremonial dinner in our culture. I normally roll the oolichan in seasoned flour and fry in lard, being careful not to overcook them. Whatever you do, if you are fortunate enough to try this local delicacy, please do not gut the fish. Cook it whole and enjoy the innards.

Nisga'a people continue to harvest the oolichan, and the fish camps become busy once per year. Not only do the Nisga'a harvest oolichan to eat fresh, we sun dry and smoke them. Most importantly, we allow vast amounts of the fish to break down, and then we cook off the oil. Oolichan oil, which we refer to a grease, or til̲x, was the single biggest trade commodity before the arrival of Europeans to our coast. Even today, our people readily await their first taste of fresh grease. We mix it in various foods for flavor, and my dad used to put it in his hair which he claimed left his hair with a nice shine.

However, not only the Nisga'a view the oolichan as an important food source. Seagulls gather by the tens of thousands. Other birds, including cormorants and eagles, flood the Nass River for their share. Pilot whales and harbor porpoises work together to round up the little oil-laden fish, and large groups of sealion porpoise through the water chase the oolichan. Another frequent visitor, the Bigfoot, are also seen wading through the river catching oolichan, often near the oolichan camps. One of the camp workers told me that he watched a family of three Bigfoot crossing the highway towards the fish camps. The fishermen tend to be more cultural-oriented than the general Nisga'a population and are often tight lipped when eluding to their experiences of Bigfoot around the oolichan camps. Today, however, visitors are more than welcome to visit the camps and talk to the fishermen. If you are in the area in late February or what we call "Pine Needles Blowing Around", or in March, visit one of the several camps just outside of Laxgalts'ap, and maybe you will get lucky and see a Bigfoot.

Laxgalts'ap (Greenville)

Simoogit Bayt Neekhl

Moving upriver from Gingolx is the community of Laxgalts'ap. Laxgalts'ap is the location of an old Nisga'a village. Back in the day, where Laxgalts'ap is located, the area was also a floodplain, and houses were raised with log pilings. Both Laxgalts'ap and Gingolx had stories from the old days of how Bigfoot would shimmy up the pilings to look in people's window. My grandmother was from Laxgalts'ap, and since the Nisga'a culture is matrilineal, Laxgalts'ap is considered my home village. I have many relatives living in Laxgalts'ap and immediately connected with the locals about Bigfoot stories and their personal experiences. The Bigfoot, known in the Nisga'a language as "Wii Xaalaxwsgum Gat" or "Big Hairy Man" in English, has been associated with Nisga'a culture for time immemorial. Wii Xaalaxwsgum Gat has always been a part of the Nisga'a culture" according to Hereditary Chief Bayt Neekhl, Jake McKay. Jake McKay was my biological grandfather's nephew. Before Jake, my grandfather held the name Bayt Neekhl. Bayt Neekhl is a Nisga'a name that refers to the long straight upright back portion of a killer whale's dorsal fin. Nisga'a names can be thousands of years old, and they are passed on during a stone-moving feast one year after a person passes on. In our culture, although Jake McKay was my grandfather's nephew, Jake would still be considered my grandfather. According to Mr. McKay, the Bigfoot had interacted with the Nisga'a people in many ways and was inextricably tied to some of their legends. Mr. McKay settled himself before discussing his knowledge of Bigfoot and the Nisga'a people. Before speaking, he seemed to brace himself as if he was passing on something extremely important to me. Obviously, he was very serious about what he was going to tell me, and I realized that he was sharing

information with me in this private setting to indicate the significance of the information he was passing on. It seemed to me to be
more than just an interview. He was the teacher, and I was the
student, and this was the lesson.

"The Bigfoot and the Nisga'a people were thought by some to
come from one and the same origin," Mr. Mckay stated. "Before the
Nisga'a came to the Nass Valley, two beings preceded them. One was
named Txeemsim, and his brother was named Logobala. They were
giants and covered with long dark hair. They both wanted the Nass
Valley and access to the Nass River but could not agree on who
should have it. They decided to settle the matter with an archery
contest. Logobola went first and hit the bulls-eye. Txeemsim went
next but after he let loose his arrow, he donned a feathered suit of the
Stellar Jay and guided the arrow, splitting the arrow of his brother.
This was the story of how Txeemsim came to possess the Nass Valley
and Nass River, while his brother took the Skeena Valley and river as
the consolation prize." Suggesting that Bigfoot and the Nisga'a people
have shared the Nass Valley for time immemorial, Mr. Mckay
discussed the significance of the Bigfoot to the Nisga'a people. "When
a person sees the Wii Xaalawsgum Gat, it means that death is close
by," recalled the Nisga'a Chief. "The Nisga'a think that the creature is
similar to humans. However, the creator gave special powers to the
creature that were not given to man such as being able to stand still
and not be seen. Some other people think that the creature has
supernatural powers."

I was interested in the idea that some people thought the Bigfoot
had supernatural powers. When asked about the subject, Mr. McKay
indicated that the Bigfoot was thought by some to be a type of Nisga'a
spiritual being known as the Naxnok. Mr. Mckay described several
Naxnok in the Nisga'a legends and the ramifications of encountering
such a being. According to the learned Chief, encounters with the
Naxnok could result in lifelong good luck if handled properly before,
during, and after the experience. In respect of the Nisga'a traditional
knowledge, I will not trivialize them by indicating what they are to
the readers of this book. However, I will tell you that the information

continues to be passed down to the Nisga'a youth, and local people continue to be wary of the cautions expressed in our stories.

When asked about his specific experiences with the Bigfoot, Mr. McKay indicated that he had not seen the creature himself but had seen evidence of its existence. In the Nisga'a community of Laxgalts'ap until the past twenty-five years, passage into the community was limited to a river crossing from a landing opposite the community. Several sightings were on or near the landing over the years, and Mr. McKay recalled a time when he and his family found some tracks of the Bigfoot, "we were getting ready to cross the river, and I had gotten out of the vehicle. I could smell it right away. It was a real strong smell. I saw some prints in the soft mud and followed them to where they came from. The tracks led back through the water, and I could see that the creature must have walked on two legs through the water, came out on the mud, and went through the bush."

Mr. McKay described another incident in which he thought he may have encountered the creature, "it was 1969," the Chief recalled. "I was in Bella Coola, and I liked to hunt in the area. I was told not to hunt in this one particular area because there were powerful things there, and the people said that there were hairy people who lived there." Mr. McKay followed the advice of the locals. However, he noticed that some other people had successfully hunted deer in the area where he was warned not to hunt. Not being one to back away from a challenge, Mr. McKay decided to go on a hunting trip in the forbidden area. "It was between September and November. I can't remember the exact date. I was sitting up high, waiting for daylight to break. My rifle was propped up against a pine tree, and I was pouring myself a hot cup of coffee from my thermos. I heard a deep- throated whistle, and I thought it could be a high-pitched moose call, a mule deer, or an elk. At that moment, I could smell an awful smell and the strength of the smell combined with the power of the animal's voice caused my body to immediately feel cold. I grabbed my rifle and started running. I could hear it crashing down the mountain towards me, and it was as if I could feel its breath on the back of my neck."

"Did you think it was a Bigfoot?" I asked. He simply nodded at me in the affirmative and continued his story. "I only ran for a few seconds and then stopped and began to back up." He indicated that he could hear the creature making strange noises and utilizing the cultural lessons he had learned as a youth, challenged the creature in the way he was taught. It seemed to have stopped moving towards him, and he started backing out of the area. He reached the bottom of the valley and promptly shot a large mule deer buck. He prayed and thanked the creator for the deer, and interestingly enough, he regularly took home game from the forbidden area.

One of the community stories came from back in the day, about a guy walking on a residential road closest to the river. It was dark in those days since there were no street lights. He was walking near where there is now a cul de sac, and he walked into something much taller than him. As he told the story, his face hit something's chest. He claimed that the thing grabbed him around his head, picked him up off the ground, and threw him. He was knocked out by the impact, and when he came too, he walked home. Now, as the story went, his wife would not have believed his story except for the fact that on the side of his forehead was a clear impression of a large thumb, and on the other side of his head were impressions of several finger tips. The next day, he went back to the spot to show other men the place where he had been grabbed. It was winter, and there was new snow early the night before, so the evidence in the snow was conclusive. Along with his footprints, there were large Bigfoot tracks. In addition, they measured the distance from where he was lifted off of the ground and where he landed. The distance was almost forty feet!

Another encounter that happened near the previous event was relayed to me. A man was walking alone on a dark foot path. The area had been cleared for housing; however, no construction had been started yet. As the man was walking, he also walked into a Bigfoot, whose eyes shined red at close range. According to this story, the Bigfoot was startled, wrapped its hand around the man's neck, and lifted him right off of the ground. The man did not attempt to fight back, and the Bigfoot put him back down and walked off in the other direction.

I had an opportunity to do a couple of consultant contracts in Laxgalts'ap as well as provide psychotherapist services there, so I had a lot of contact with many of the residents. One resident told me about his fishing experience with his brother. He said his brother dropped him off near a creek where they had set out their fishing net. After taking the fish off the net, he walked to the creek to wash his hands. He was surprised to see several very large human-shaped footprints near the creek and he could smell a strong odor in the area. He also found similar tracks in the area several years later.

One of the most entertaining stories I heard was from the community of Laxgalt'ap was of an older man who had been out on the land and was quietly surveying the area. At first, he noticed a strange smell and found it difficult to avoid gagging. He noticed some movement and ducked down to avoid being seen. He was quite surprised to see an upright walking creature at a slight angle away from him. The creature had dark fur covering its whole back, and its hair seemed thick and long. What he noticed next truly shocked him: a baby Bigfoot was hanging off the large creature's shoulder. The man who witnessed the mother and child said that the child had no difficulty hanging on during the bumpy ride on his mother's back. The man said he was close enough to see the baby urinating down the mother's hairy back.

When they were putting in the highway extension from Laxgalts'ap to Gingolx, I asked some of the highway workers if they had experienced anything strange. At first, they looked at each other and seemed reluctant to say anything. They then told me that some creatures they assumed they were Bigfoot, but they could never see the whole animal, only their red glowing eyes, were rolling large boulders over the rock walls onto the highway and throwing smaller rocks toward them. They only did this at night. While the eyes moved from a standing position to a squatting position quite regularly, the men could never see their bodies. When the road was completed one year later, a couple who wanted to remain anonymous told me they were walking along the highway. They were busy talking to each other, but when they both looked up, they saw a Bigfoot in the middle of the road. They quickly turned back and made haste back to Laxgalts'ap.

Another fellow from Laxgalts'ap told me about an incident where he and several friends had been working in the forest and were returning on a well-used trail to their small boat. The trail curved around the side of a large hill, and this particular fellow wanted to reach the boat sooner, and he began walking straight down the hill along-side the creek while his mates continued to take the trail. He indicated that as soon as he reached the bottom of the hill and neared the riverside, he saw someone hunched over the side of the boat going through their gear. He indicated that he thought one of the guys beat him to the boat, and he was interested as to what it was. As he neared the boat, the Bigfoot looked up, and this fellow realized that he was looking at a Bigfoot. The creature ran away, and that was the end of his story.

Another interesting story was told to me by a younger man who had been out gathering shellfish with several other young men. During the nights, they slept in the bow of the boat, under cover from the weather. The boat was tied up near the river's edge, and the conditions were reasonably calm. In the middle of the night, the men heard something walking towards their boat through the water. They heard the creature "wading" toward them through several feet of water. Suddenly, their boat tipped sideways, and some creature pulled into the boat and began to rummage through their gear. The men huddled together near the rear of the stern pointed a loaded rifle at the door of the cabin. The creature did not try to open the door, and he slipped off the boat in a similar manner as he entered.

Between Gitwinksihlkw and Laxgalts'ap, there is a thirty-minute drive in which there are numerous reports of Bigfoot being seen. The first place of interest is the waterguage. It is a place along the highway where people used to mark where the water had risen to in the old days. It was normal at one time for the roads to be cut off by flooding during the spring and fall months. Now, there are only a few places along the Nisga'a Highway where flooding occurs and is usually pass-able with a truck. Two different people have described seeing a white-haired Bigfoot crossing the highway and running up the steep slope on the eastern side of the highway near the waterguage.

The next stop along the highway for regular sightings is at Ksiidin Creek. I know this area well, as it was our family's traditional fishing area. A couple of fellows had asked me if it was OK if they put a fishing net out at that spot. Since we were not using it, I told them to go ahead. A couple of weeks later, I ran into one of them, and he told me they had packed up and wouldn't be going there again. He told me that while they were pulling in their net from shore, something on the trail to their left started screaming at them. A couple of years later, another fellow, came to see me and told me they tried fishing at the same spot. When they returned to check their net, it had been pulled up on shore and left in a pile, and the fish was gone. At first, they thought it was me or someone in our family or that it may have been the fisheries officers. When they began letting the net drift out, something screamed at them from the trail and threw a piece of log at them, almost hitting them. They ran out of there and left their net behind. He vowed never to go there again.

I have taken many trips since to Ksiidin Creek and have looked for tracks around the trail beside where our family used to fish. I had also looked around the field of tall grass where we park vehicles but had not seen any real evidence other than a walking trail. However, the guy who had seen a Bigfoot running on the lava beds came to where I worked one day to attend a board meeting and told me that he had seen three Bigfoot walking in that small field at Ksiidin Creek just one week before.

There is a long straight stretch along the highway, and a couple of people have told me that they have seen logs being thrown onto the highway, but they hadn't seen what had done it. A co-worker of mine had been driving along that stretch of the highway, and something had thrown a sizeable boulder at her vehicle, shattering one of her back-seat windows. I was told a similar story by three separate people, not only seeing logs being thrown on the road but also a large

Bigfoot emerging to cross the highway. The most interesting of these stories was told to me by a Nisga'a chief who did not want to be identified. As he began to describe his experience, he paused as if experiencing some residue of discomfort from the memory. He began describing a trip in his pick-up truck, at which time he was following his nephew, who was driving in his own pick-up truck. The two vehicles were approximately fifteen minutes out of their home community of Laxgalts'ap when the Chief saw his nephew pull off to the side of the road in a hurried fashion. He, of course, pulled over himself and waited for his nephew to get out of his vehicle. After a minute or two, he became impatient and got out of his own truck, went over to his nephew's window, and knocked on the window. He indicated that his nephew was slow to react, and when able to pull his white-knuckled hands off the steering wheel, he slowly rolled down his window. The Chief indicated that he could see that his nephew was in shock, and he asked him what had happened. The nephew pointed to the side of the road in front of his vehicle, where a medium-sized log and some extending branches obstructed the left shoulder and portion of the road. The chief claimed that his nephew told him the log had just sailed across the road and landed in its current position. The nephew told him that after the log landed on the shoulder of the road, a large Bigfoot followed behind and crossed the highway in front of him. Another fellow told me of a harrowing experience that he had on the same stretch of highway. He and his wife had been travelling down the road during the night when he pulled off to the side of the highway. He was busy doing something when his wife began making inaudible sounds and pointing to his side window. He looked over and watched something walking alongside his truck. He indicated that it must have been very tall as all he could see was the top of its legs and its waist. It then crossed the highway before it got in front of his truck.

Down the road from this stretch of highway is a logging road that goes down into an area called Ginlulak. Several years ago, the government sent a survey team down there to begin surveying for logging blocks. After a week, the surveyors emerged and vowed not to go back there. When the locals asked what had happened, they indicated that something was living there and did not want them in there surveying.

More recently, I had begun receiving reports of encounters near the McKay Bridge, a relatively long bridge spanning a wide part of the Nass River. A friend of mine told me that she and a friend had stopped at the end of the bridge at night so she could relieve herself. While squatting down in the bush, she heard footsteps from a large two-footed creature walking towards them. While running out of the bush and to their vehicle, they could hear the creature running behind them and snapping off branches of the trees. They did not see the creature come out of the forest.

A cousin of mine and her friend were traveling back to Laxgalts'ap after attending a meeting in Terrace. It was dark, and they were traveling near the McKay Bridge. She had to slam on the brakes after she noticed some movement on the highway. She and her friend watched something very tall cross the highway in front of them. She indicated that because they were so close, they could only see its two hairy long legs and not the upper part of its body.

I had heard of a local police officer who had seen a Bigfoot around the bridge on two occasions. When I was talking to my cousin, who had seen the Bigfoot cross the road in front of her, I asked her if she had heard about the officer seeing the Bigfoot. She told me that she had spoken to the officer, and he told her he had seen two of them on different occasions but didn't know if it was the same Bigfoot or two different ones. Another cousin of mine was a flagger for a road crew, and they were doing some work along the road around two hundred meters from the bridge. One morning, as they were putting out the cones and warning signs, he heard a large initial crash in the forest, and then he heard something running through the forest, breaking tree branches as it ran. He also told me that BC Hydro was investigating damage to some of the hydro poles, as some of the poles appear to have been cracked as if they were repeatedly struck by something.

A couple of months after he told me about his experience, I was driving late at night near my property, heading up to the area around Bigfoot Road. We saw someone pull off the side of the highway, and I stopped to see if everything was okay. His name was Spooner, and he had gotten a flat tire on the Nass Forest Service Road. He had been driving with a flat tire, and his rim gave out. I offered him a ride to Gitlaxt'aamiks where he had friends who could help him. While driving, he asked what we were doing so late (it was 1:00 am) and we told him we were looking for Bigfoot. Without missing a beat, he said, "It's down by Greenville." Slightly amused, I asked him what he was talking about. He said that he and his wife were driving to Laxgalts'ap one week earlier and saw a tall, skinny Bigfoot standing beside a hydro pole. Well, the truth is I had to have a chuckle at that. I told him that Bigfoots are not skinny or not that I have ever heard of. He was a bit miffed at my response but maintained it was either a skinny Bigfoot or a skinny grizzly standing up.

The next day, because of the recent sighting, I talked my girlfriend into driving down to the McKay Bridge at night. We saw nothing that night, so we decided to try again the next night and then the next. In all, we went eleven nights in a row at varying times between 9:00 pm and 1:00 am. On the twelfth day, we drove to Terrace to pick up a smaller hand-held spotlight and went to the McKay Bridge again. I pulled up alongside the highway approximately 100 meters from the start of the bridge. Marie pulled out our new spotlight, and I said to roll the window down and shine the spotlight into the forest at the same place where my cousin heard the Bigfoot crashing through the forest. As she was about to roll down the window, I noticed a large dark shape at the edge of my headlights. Since we were parked on an upward slope, the headlights shone over the dark shape. I asked Marie, "What the hell is that?" It was very windy that night, and you could see that whatever was at the edge of the headlights, the wind appeared to be moving part of it. Marie remarked that it looked like a big bush with the leaves blowing back and forth. I remarked that it looked like a large bush, but there were no big bushes along the highway, only small ones. I put the car into drive and slowly moved forward. I got about five feet before two long arms emerged from the body and reached over the bank. The Bigfoot's butt raised into the air, and for a second, it resembled the shape of a triangle, and within the blink of an eye, it moved over the bank in one swift motion. I quickly sped up to where it had been squatting, which only took a few seconds. Marie was somewhat incapacitated with fear, but I yelled to her to use the window button to lower the window and shine the spotlight down into the forest. When the window rolled down, we could hear it walking into the forest. What is interesting is that there is at least forty feet between the top of the bank and the ditch at the bottom, which was filled with water because the river was high that year. In addition, from the ditch to the forest was another forty feet. In the time it took to reach where it had been squatting and the time it took to roll down the window, the Bigfoot was already walking into the forest. When Marie turned on the spotlight, the Bigfoot took off running directly away from us and breaking tree branches as it did. That was quite the adrenaline rush.

We waited for a couple of minutes, and although still a bit shaky, we crossed the McKay bridge, drove for about five kilometers, and turned around at a logging road. We decided to go home as that was the first Bigfoot Marie had ever seen, and we accomplished our goal of seeing the McKay Bridge Bigfoot. However, halfway back to the bridge, I was approaching a corner but was still on a short, straight stretch. My headlights somewhat illuminated the upcoming corner, and at the right side of the road was a tall, skinny female Bigfoot! Her body was slightly facing towards me because of where she was standing on the corner, and her upper body was slightly turned towards me because she was looking at us. The guy with the flat tire we had helped out was not lying or exaggerating; this female Bigfoot had shoulders approximately the same width as her hips and was standing straight up. Now look, I do not want to be rude, and I have no idea what is considered attractive in the Bigfoot species, but she was ugly in terms of human looks. She had this incredibly long face, and her cheekbones were very high on her face but very small compared to the length of her face. If I were to make any comparative reference, her face looked like a witch's face that one might see in a

Hollywood movie. Although she appeared to be looking directly at me, I could not see her eyes. They seemed to be deeply sunken into her face. I immediately recognized that her appearance strongly resembled the male Bigfoot's facial features in the photograph I saw that was taken at the Gingolx cemetery. We looked at each other for a couple of seconds, and then she quickly moved across the road and was gone. Interestingly, although she moved extremely quickly, suggesting she was running, her arms remained at her sides, and she remained perfectly upright. When I tell people this particular story, I describe her crossing the highway in a cartoonish running motion, as if she was effortlessly moving at high speed without the exaggerated body motion that human beings have. It would have been nice to have seen her legs moving, but there was no such luck.

Gitwinksihlkw (People of the Lizard)

One of the Nisga'a communities is named Gitwinksihlkw (The People of the Lizards) but used to be called Canyon City. In previous times, lizards used to live in that area, however, they have not been seen for a long time and are feared to have become extinct. A steel and concrete bridge now provides access to the community. However, in past times, visitors and citizens had to cross a narrow suspension bridge hovering over the swirling and sometimes violent Nass River. Gitwinksihlkw is located on the western side of the Nass River adjacent to the lava beds. The Nisga'a highway corridor winds its way through the recently established provincial park, which cuts through the heart of the lava beds. The road leading to the Gitwinksihlkw bridge was placed through the edge of the lava flow, and that road connects with the main Nisga'a highway.

As I indicated earlier, the Nass Valley is home to Canada's most recent volcano, which contains some of the most spectacular lava bed formations in Canada. In the middle of winter, during the coldest temperatures, steam rises off the lava bed, created by the natural hot water springs that circulate beneath the rock. The lava beds have been a hot spot for Bigfoot sightings. Several people had told me they had seen Bigfoot on or near the lava-beds, some closer to Gitwinksih-lkw, and some a bit farther away. These are their stories.

New to the Nass Valley and on their first trip through the lava-beds, a family I knew quite well had a visual encounter with Bigfoot. Like many others on their first trip through the lava-beds, they slowed down to take in the breath-taking scenery. Off to the right, when entering from the direction of Terrace, the edge of the lava-beds is within view, and trees line its edge. As they slowly drove through the open area of the lava-beds, my future colleague's wife spotted what she thought was a grizzly bear and asked her husband to stop the car. She was the one who related the story to me. At some distance, she noticed what looked like a large dark animal running upright towards a stand of trees. She pointed out to her husband where the animal had run to, and they could see that it was attempting to hide behind one of the larger trees. In her words, the animal walked over to the largest of the trees and began hugging it. I did not even make a remark at this point, but she must have read something on my face, and she claimed, "yes, it was hugging a tree." She said it was not a grizzly bear because it had human-shaped arms except that they were all hairy and extremely long. She indicated that the arms went around the whole tree and that you could see its fingers. When I asked her husband about that event a couple of years later, he just looked at me and said nothing.

In that same area of the lava-beds, one of the board of directors where I worked told me that he saw a Bigfoot running across that portion of the lava-beds. I know another fellow who saw a young Bigfoot walking down a side road just before the spot where the other witnesses saw the larger Bigfoot. His encounter with a young one is related to a personal story I will tell later. Needless to say, I always drive slowly in that area, but I have never seen a Bigfoot there.

One of the jobs I did in the Nass Valley was coordinating vocational and technical programs for the local post-secondary institute in Gitwinksihlkw. In my first stint with the organization, I was in charge of the institute newsletter. I used to pass my time on the computer, sometimes developing comical news stories and placing funny pictures to illustrate an educational program I was coordinating.

When this event happened, there was a neck-and-neck race between George Bush and Al Gore in the USA presidential election. Although Canadian, I was hoping Gore would win as Bush and his camp seemed to be pro-conflict versus pro-peace. One of the training programs I set up was for the community of Gitwinksihlkw. I had set up a flagging course, and the training took place on the entrance road to the Gitwinksihlkw bridge. On the day of the course, I drove down to the site to take some pictures for my report. The vehicles traveling into and out of Gitwinksihlkw had to go past the flaggers, and I felt some pride in knowing I helped to make the training a reality. I pulled over and spoke with the course trainer and some students. I pulled out my camera and took several pictures of the trainer and trainees, as well as some pictures of the surrounding lava-beds. I jokingly thought that I might capture a picture of a Bigfoot without even knowing it.

When I got back to my office, the self-joke about getting a picture of Bigfoot got me thinking, and I decided to fool around on the computer and place a picture of the Patterson Bigfoot into one of my lava-bed pictures. I made what looked like a ballot card with Bush and Gore's name on it and shrunk it. I changed the orientation of the paper and placed it into the hand of the Bigfoot. When I showed people the picture on my computer, I would pretend to notice the paper in his hand and zoom in. On the card would be the names of the two candidates and a checkmark beside Gore.

A couple of years later, I was talking to a woman from the community of Gitwinksihlkw, and she began telling me about a Bigfoot experience she had on the lava-beds. She told me about when she saw a Bigfoot near the greenbelt edge of the lava fields, which at this time was relatively close by. She said that she was eating her lunch, and when she stood up to put her lunch bag into her pack sack, she saw a Bigfoot stand up that had been squatting down on the lava. The Bigfoot turned away from her and began walking toward the edge of the lava-bed. Within approximately 30 seconds, it had reached the trees. She described the creature as very tall and very large. She described it as walking like an ape and a man. She indicated that it had dark fur or hair and blended well with the local surroundings. Although this story was not unusual, and I felt that the person was a credible witness, what she told me next stopped me in my tracks. She told me that she saw it when she was taking a break from a training course that she was taking at the time. I asked her what type of training, and she told me it was a flagging course she had taken on the road entering the Gitwinksihlkw Bridge. I told her that I had set up that training program, and she stated that she already knew that. I then told her the story of the pictures I took on that day and how I placed the Patterson picture in one of the lava bed pictures depicting a voting Bigfoot. Imagine our surprise with each other's stories, one fiction and one reality on the same day and at the same place.

Several months ago, I attended a settlement feast in Gitlaaxt'aamiks. A settlement feast is put on by the Clan House of a person who has recently passed away. I noticed some men from Gitwinksihlkw there, and one of them was pretty anxious to tell what he had seen several days earlier. He said several people were traveling with him in his vehicle crossing the bridge when he glanced down and saw three Bigfoot walking along the river bank: two adults and one younger one. This bridge will be brought up later in this book, and let me warn you, it will be a story that you will find hard to believe!

One of the hotbed areas for Bigfoot sightings in the Nass Valley is along the Nisga'a Highway but within the Lava Bed Memorial Provincial Park. It is called Memorial as the largest of the Nisga'a villages was once located within its central area. The pyroclastic flow from the volcanic eruption moved too quickly for the residents to move to safety, and approximately 2500 Nisga'a perished in the blast. In some areas of the lava beds, the forest has begun to reclaim the lava floor. Vetter Creek winds through the lava bed, and the forest lines its path. Vetter Creek is a beautiful area and is one of the stops on the highway self-guided road tour through the valley. It is also a great place for picking pine mushrooms. It has some of the thickest moss in the Nass Valley, and the creek flows with icy cold water. The Vetter Creek area is a favorite place for mushroom pickers. However, it is not a favorite with the local Search and Rescue. Many pickers have lost themselves in the intricate web of mushroom patches surrounding the area. A couple of friends of mine, Doug and Shawn, are two seasoned mushroom pickers who love to pick the area. Well, they did love to pick the area. A couple of years ago, they came by my place and told me they had climbed to the top of the area hoping to find the mother lode of mushrooms. They had never been up that far before, and what they saw made their blood run cold. They came to a place where two rock walls came together but had an opening between them. They could not see through the opening or what was behind it. What frightened them was that approximately two hundred young pine trees in front of the opening had been broken over at about four feet. All the trees were broken in the same direction: towards the forest where they just walked out. Now, Shawn and Doug have not seen a Bigfoot, but they instinctively realized that they had come across the lair of one. They beat a hasty retreat and told me they would never be picking at Vetter Creek again.

A few others have told me stories of encountering Bigfoot near Vetter Creek. One particular story involved a group of avid bingo players. "We were coming home from bingo, and there were four of us in the car. We saw the thing the next day, too, but there were a different four of us that day. This night it was dark, and you know how it is around there. We were going around eighty, and it just came out of nowhere. The headlights showed a large ape-like thing, and it looked like it was going to walk in front of the car" (the car was a small white Toyota). When I asked the witness what she did, she claimed that all the vehicle occupants started screaming simultaneously, and she hit her brakes and shielded her face from the expected impact. The car screeched to a halt, and she cried hysterically along with her confused passengers. Thankfully she did not hit the Bigfoot. Apparently, she did not learn her lesson, and the next night was traveling back home from bingo with one passenger from the night before and two different passengers. They were purposely traveling more slowly along the same stretch of road when, as if on cue, there was the Bigfoot walking along the side of the dark highway once again. There was no need to hit the brakes this time, and they continued to drive.

I also interviewed a woman who was traveling past Vetter Creek in a school bus when she was younger. The school bus was full with her classmates when a Bigfoot crossed the highway in front of them. The students gathered up to the front of the bus to look at it. Interestingly, I brought this up with the bus driver, but she looked at me and did not say a word. I inferred that she did not want to talk about it.

The lava-beds begin at the end of Lava Lake. A friend of mine used to take her grandchildren to the lake, and they would explore its perimeter. On two separate occasions, something began tossing pebbles at them. As a spiritual person, she prayed telling the Bigfoot they meant no harm. She said that after she prayed, the pebble tossing stopped. A couple of days later they returned to explore. Soon after, the pebble tossing started. However, the stones began to get larger this time, and she suspected that the Bigfoot was telling her to get lost.

One of the Board of Directors where I worked, the same guy who had seen the Bigfoot running on the lava-beds, approached me one day before a board meeting. "Did you hear about the Lake?" he asked. He told me that some Californian tourists had come down to his community of Gingolx two days earlier and told a fantastic tale about their experience with a local Bigfoot. They first inquired whether such creatures lived in the Nass Valley, which they found affirmative. As the story went, the tourists were traveling alongside the Lava Lake highway corridor, which had recently been upgraded and paved in the summer of 2003. They saw two large creatures swimming across the lake and decided to pull over. They assumed that the creatures were moose due to their large heads and the fact that they were swimming at a fast rate. They continued to watch the moose until they reached the other side of the lake, and that was when their story took a twist. They indicated that the creatures reached the other side;

however, when they stood up and walked out of the water, both creatures walked on two legs and were not moose but were two Bigfoot.

On the other end of the lake, far more sightings are reported. In fact, sightings had been reported for decades in that area. My grandfather used to trade with a gold miner who lived in that area sixty years ago. He would tell my grandfather and uncle that he often ran into a Bigfoot there and actually got used to it being around. People will often stop me and tell me that they or someone they know recently saw a Bigfoot on or near the highway where the lake begins. A friend of mine stopped his car at the pull-off, where a large sign introduces and welcomes visitors to the provincial park. His sixteen-year-old son got out of the car and stepped down the bank to the shore of the lake. After a few seconds, he hurriedly came back. My friend was alarmed as the natural brown color in his son's face was gone and, in its place, an ashen appearance. He asked him what was wrong. His son replied that he saw something down there. When my friend asked him if it was a bear, he said it wasn't. He asked again what it was, but his son would only say he did not know what it was. His son was quite rattled by it, but further questioning did not result in him divulging what he saw. Later that evening, he overheard his son talking to his other son. He heard his other son, asking, "are you sure that is what you saw?" That was the last my friend heard of the subject. Three weeks later (about three years ago), I was coming home late from Terrace, and I came around a bend on the highway just before the pull-off spot. Off to my left was something standing behind the cement barrier and slightly down the bank. It was getting dark, and the trees obscured it, but I could see two bright but deep red wide-set eyes looking directly at me. I had heard about Bigfoot having red eyes, but I dismissed it (guilty of disqualifying the positive). Later, I will discuss three other examples of red eyes, but now I will continue on to the last of Nisga'a villages.

Gitlaxt'aamiks

The Nisga'a community of Gitlaxt'aamiks is located approximately ninety kilometers north of Terrace. There are around twelve hundred residents in the community, which sprawls along the hillside and is located on the northeastern ridge alongside the lava beds. The community was relocated in 1963 from Old Aiyansh due to flooding, which was located across the Nass River. I had lived in Gitlax̱t'aamiks for several years growing up and also spent several additional summers there with my grandparents. When I was thirteen, my family built and operated a restaurant there. Part of the restaurant was held up with long log pilings as a small ravine was between my grandparent's home and the restaurant. After the restaurant closed for the evening, my brothers, uncle, and I would often stay at the restaurant and play a few rounds of cards. One night, I went home after we closed, and my brother Steven and uncle Herb stayed to play cards in the restaurant. Out of nowhere, we heard screaming coming from the restaurant, which continued up the road to the house. My brother and uncle came running in and out of breath. My grandparents were alarmed and asked what happened. They said that when playing cards at a table beside a window nearest the ravine, something had climbed the log piling and was peering through the window at them; it had big red glowing eyes. Since no one really talked about Bigfoot in those days, we chalked it up to some kind of spirit, which made much more sense then.

Much later, when I was an adult and moved back to the Gitlaxt'aamkiks, I had my second Bigfoot sighting. However, I am saving that story for another chapter. However, my wife and I were not the only ones to have seen a Bigfoot around the community that year. I was speaking with a woman who said that she was driving past the nurse's apartments down the road from my place. It was getting dark, and a large Bigfoot stood out of the ditch. The ditch was only two and a half feet deep. She slammed on her brakes, and the Bigfoot stepped out of the ditch and onto the road. She claimed that the Bigfoot was white. I asked her whether her headlights might have made it look white. She looked straight into my eyes and firmly reiterated that it was white. She said it, and then she started walking towards her car. She had her children with her and stepped on the gas pedal, swerving around the Bigfoot. A couple of other people from the community told me they saw the Bigfoot walking on the community roads, but their comments were in passing, and I could not interview them for a more in-depth discussion.

A woman who lived across the street from me shared an experience she had approximately a month after I had mine. She said it was a foggy evening, and she looked out her curtains and saw a tall man standing beside a power pole. Because of the fog, she couldn't see him clearly, but he was slightly swaying, and she thought he might be intoxicated. After approximately half an hour, she heard screaming and banging on her door. She recognized her daughter's voice and opened the door to which her daughter and her friend ran in, still screaming and crying. Once they calmed down, they said they were coming up the driveway when a large Bigfoot walked out of their garage and past the two girls. They said the Bigfoot did not even look at them but stared straight ahead. The woman then realized that the swaying man she thought was intoxicated must have been the Bigfoot.

I talked to a respected hunter in the community and he told me a story about driving around the community one evening. He had taken a drive to the cemetery in the waning hours of daylight. He indicated that he had seen a very large creature, which resembled a large ape, standing beside a large spruce tree. In the reflection of his headlights, he said that the color of the eyes appeared to be red.

I had spoken to an older couple in the community who told me that they had watched more than one Bigfoot interacting in their back yard. The Bigfoot had left evidence in terms of large footprints and they showed the footprints to others. Similar to where I lived in the community, the older couple's house was backed along a greenbelt.

While most of the people I have interviewed over the years have been adults, a thirteen-year-old girl, a niece of mine, wanted to tell me about her and her friend's encounter the prior year. She indicated that her and several friends had walked down to the local store to get some ice cream. It had already grown dark, but they had a flashlight and were sticking to the lit roads. They played hide and seek on their way back home, hiding behind local shrubs and a small office building along the road. After some time of playing the game, the group re-organized along-side the road and began walking once again. They did not get far when one of the children pointed the flashlight near a large sign. According to the girl telling the story, the boy stopped and said, "What the heck is that?" My niece raised her eyes and said that a Bigfoot was standing alongside the sign, only partially obscured by the wood holding up the sign. She indicated that the head of the Bigfoot was as tall as the top of the sign, about eight feet high. By now, the whole group had seen the creature and had stopped walking towards it. At some point, the group became collectively terrified and turned and ran back down the road and took another route home. I spoke to the mother of one of the children about the incident, and I was quite surprised by her response. She readily agreed that the children's experience was interesting, but she quickly began describing her experience when she first came to the Nass Valley. She stated, "when I was young, I traveled with my grand-father in a vehicle near the cemetery one day. The windows were rolled down, and a slight breeze drifted through the car. We passed a section where a very strong odor of rotting fish permeated the air. My grandfather quickly told me that the smell was from a Bigfoot, and to be careful around that area."

Lorene Plante

I interviewed a local Matriarch from the Nisga'a community of Gitlaxt'aamiks. She told me a story of her experience with a Bigfoot while she was picking mushrooms with her niece. I entered her small gift shop specializing in traditional and modern Native art. She seemed happy and excited to tell her story. Her eyes sparkled as she settled in to tell the story. "It was in the year 2000," she said. "I was picking mushrooms on the Grease Trail, up by where it comes out on the Hoodoo." Hardly able to contain her excitement, she blurted out, "It had silver-tipped fur." I respectfully asked her to back up and describe what kind of day it was. "It was kind of a cloudy day," she stated. "I was with my niece, and we were going into the forest, and we found a large pile of smelly shit. We were careful not to step in it. My niece was moving ahead of me because she is taller and has long legs. When she gets in front of me and I can't see her, I call out, 'yoo hoo Merna, where are you?' She usually responded by whistling a short whistle like a bird."

"How long were you picking mushrooms before you seen the Bigfoot?" I asked.

"I was picking for about fifteen minutes near the road when I called out, 'yoo hoo Merna.' I heard a whistle. It was below me, and within a few minutes I heard the whistle behind me. I couldn't figure out how she got behind me so fast, and I started picking in that direction."

"Is that when you saw the Bigfoot?" I asked.

"No," she said. "First, I smelled this horrible smell, so gross I couldn't identify it."

"Did it smell like rotten meat?" I asked.

"It smelled like shit, like shit rubbed all over," she stated. "I checked my shoes for shit, and there wasn't any, and that is when I got a feeling like someone was watching me. I called out to Merna and immediately noticed a whistling sound coming from very close by. I turned in a circle, looking for her. I turned to the whistling, and noticed something wiggling on either side of a tree. I then saw its hands holding the tree, like it was hugging it. And I was holding a tree, yelling for Merna at the same time."

"How far away was it?" I asked.

"About from here over to there," she indicated, pointing to the length of her door to the opposite end of the room. We estimated the distance to be about twenty-five to thirty feet away.

I was surprised by the short distance and asked, "That close?"

"Yes," she stated. "It was very close. It was behind a tree with black and white bark, like you know?"

"An alder," I suggested.

"I think so", she said. I seen its ears moving, hugging a tree. Its eyes were oval shaped."

"Are you sure they were oval-shaped or was the fur shaped at an upward angle to make it look like the eyes were oval?" I asked. With great certainty, she stated, "The eyes were oval." I drew a simple picture indicating a large pair of oval eyes. She claimed that the eyes were not large: they just had an oval shape. She quickly tried to distract me from the drawing and stated, "My grandmother told me never to look in the eyes of a Sasquatch because I could get hypnotized. It had a bare chest."

"Like a gorilla?" I asked.

"Yes." She continued, "It had silver-tipped fur. I think it was an old one. His ears were twitching, and he had longer ears."

"Like moose ears?" I asked.

"No, like our ears except a little longer upward," she said, slightly annoyed by my question.

"How tall was it?" I asked.

"It was about seven feet," she replied. "It was hugging a tree, trying to camouflage itself, but I could see its hands. I started to back away and began running backward towards the road. By the time I reached the road, I turned around and saw a car, and I tried to catch up with it." Watching Lorene tell the story, I noticed her exhibiting signs of fear. "Backing up?" I asked.

"I ran backward because my granny told me never to turn my back on a Sasquatch." I started running opposite where the car passed, and I saw a large pile of cut wood. I was going to climb to the top of the pile when I remembered that people have seen Sasquatch standing on logs on the beach." With a spry smile on her face, she said, "I stood there, and I heard a loud thumping sound."

"It was chasing you?" I asked. Somewhat irritated at my interruption, she continued, "No, I heard a loud thumping sound, and I concentrated on listening to where it was coming from." She paused and exclaimed, "It was my own heart" and laughed loudly. "When I realized it was not following me, I called for Merna, and she hollered back. I ran to her, and she claimed that I looked totally white. I asked her to leave, and she wanted to stay longer. I yelled at her and told her that we were going home immediately. When I got into the car, I immediately fell fast asleep, which I couldn't understand. For six weeks, I had problems. I couldn't go into my bedroom alone. I was scared. I told people I had seen a creature I didn't understand."

"What did you do?" I asked.

"My friend, an elder, phoned me and told me to go into the bedroom with the phone. She said a prayer, and I felt it go away when she was finished."

"That was an interesting story," I exclaimed.

"That wasn't the end," she declared. Some other pickers went up the next day and found large -shaped tracks, and others found interwoven branches up high that looked like a roof had been made for sleeping under."

I thanked Lorene and asked her for a card. I indicated that I would print her card in the book in exchange for her story. Unfortunately, Lorene passed away a couple of weeks ago. If you get a chance and you find yourself in Gitlaxt'aamiks (formerly known as New Aiyansh), stop by her shop, and maybe she'll tell you the story.

In addition to the Wii Xaalaxwsguum Gat or large hairy man, two other types of Bigfoot are a part of Nisga'a culture. One type is known as the Hagwil Lok or Beast Man. It is the kind my mother talked about who was turning the door handle when she was visiting her grandparents in Gitwinksihlkw, and it is the Bigfoot who interacts with people in a cheeky or destructive manner. My mother also told me stories of when she was a child in which large animals crashing through the forest were interpreted as the Hagwil Lok by the Elders. No one dared step outside when the Hagwil Lok was around.

The third type of creature often reported through Nisga'a premodern and modern times is the "Waadimhl". This is a female Bigfoot who sometimes comes to the villages when her children are ill. Their children often cry early in the mornings, and after some days, the mother will begin wailing; both cries sound like the sounds that humans make. This scenario gave rise to the story that if you manage to take her baby away from her and then give her back, good luck will follow you for the rest of your life. Some stories say that even if you pretend you have taken the child and then returned it, good luck will follow, but only if you heed the warning of not turning your back to her. It is said that she can cover ground so fast that by the time you even start running, she is on you, clawing up your back.

The cultural information provided to me by Simoogit Bayt Neekhl and Lorene is an oral historical record of the Nisga'a interaction with the Bigfoot. The phenomenon of Bigfoot did not begin with the arrival of European peoples but began when Indigenous Peoples settled in North America. The Nisga'a are as knowledgeable about their territories as any comparable land owners in the world. Their intimate knowledge of the land and resources compiled over many generations is a testament to the strength of their oral tradition. The knowledge presented and shared by the elders has as much validity as any historical facts preserved in written form. In this author's opinion, much could be learned from the historical perspective of the First Nations people. As I move to the next chapter, I will begin recounting my first Bigfoot encounter, which was also the beginning of my interest in Bigfoot and the start of my research endeavor.

4

CYCLOPS AND THE WORLD'S WORST BIGFOOT RESEARCHER

One day in 2000, my daughter Christina and I were out on the Grease Trail cutting smokehouse wood. The Grease Trail is an ancient trade route used by the Nisga'a people and people from other First Nations as a travel route for the trade of oolichan grease and other trade goods. Christina and I were sharing some quality time working together to cut and pack the wood that I used for smoking salmon. We used a particular type of cottonwood that needs to be aged to produce the kind of smoke that gives a smooth taste to the fish. Christina was a strong young girl who enjoyed the outdoors almost as much as me. We were almost finished gathering the wood when my dog Casey began barking incessantly at a large spruce tree approximately 25 feet away from us. The spot we were gathering the wood was along a winding creek. Although it was slightly past mid-afternoon, the surrounding underbrush and position of the surrounding trees cast a dark shadow around the spruce tree that Casey was barking at. The bottom branches of the spruce tree were about five feet off of the ground, and the underbrush was about five feet high, and combined with the shadows, I could not see much beneath the tree even though I was straining my eyes to see anything in the darkness. The first time Casey started barking, I could not see anything and continued to finish chain-sawing the cottonwood log. The second time she started barking, I shut off the saw. Casey was a beautiful pit bull, and she was very protective. She was also fearless, and on numerous occasions, she went right after black bears and grizzly bears that had gotten too close to us when we were picking mushrooms. She foolishly left my side in the forest one time, lured away by a male wolf. I had stopped by the mushroom shacks and told people to call me if someone found Casey. I received a call two hours later and was informed that Herb Hewen found her on the Grease Trail at kilometer six. I found Herb at Nass Camp with Casey. He told me that he came around a corner at kilometer six, and Casey was backed up against a rock cliff wall, fighting off a pack of wolves one by one. Herb jumped out, fired off a couple of shots, and scared the wolves away. Before he knew it, Casey ran behind him and jumped into the passenger seat. Casey was the finest dog I ever had. While I have introduced Herb as a hero at this point in the story, he becomes a more important figure later on, but you will have to wait for that.

I noticed that Casey was standing about ten feet away from the tree incessantly barking, and this concerned me because of her past tendency to confront animals such as bears more aggressively. In addition, she was looking up when she was barking which was odd. My better sense kicked in, and I called my daughter over to me. I looked again at the tree, and I was surprised to see a hovering light just underneath the bottom branches of the spruce tree. Foolishly and in terror, my first thought was "Alien!". After watching for a few seconds, I realized that idea was silly, and I then thought it must be a person with some kind of large pen light, as I estimated the light to be the diameter of a quarter. Again, after a few seconds, I realized that idea was absurd as who would be hiding in the bush watching me gather wood. I thought for a second that it might be a person smoking a cigarette, and I had a rush of fear. However, I could not smell any smoke and quickly dismissed that idea. That was when I realized that it was not an alien, penlight, or cigarette; it was the reflection from the eye of some animal, which was even more terrifying to me.

Although we were not far from the bushy area where the animal was watching us, the truck was even closer. In addition, Casey was between us and the animal, so I calmed down. I pointed at the eye and asked my daughter if she could see it. At first, she could not see it, so I exaggerated the pointing to draw her attention. She then said that she could see it, but the creature seemed to react to my exaggerated pointing. The creature ducked down into the darker shadowed bushes and appeared to be trying to hide. I lowered my hand, followed the eye reflection with my finger, and began pointing it out to my daughter. Immediately, the creature shifted its weight towards the tree trunk, trying to hide in the denser bush. I still struggle with this because it was so startling to watch it shift to the side, but as it did, I could make out a set of extremely wide shoulders, but I could not see ahead. In a way, it was rather comical because the more the creature tried to hide in the low brush where it seemed darker, the more brightly illuminated the eye appeared! When I dropped my hand in astonishment and stopped pointing, the creature immediately rose again to its full height. At that point, I realized that it knew I was pointing at it and that it must have been very tall. When I first saw it, all I could see was its eye, but now I could see the enormous outline of its upper body. I suspected it might be a Bigfoot and immediately felt a wave of fear. However, something strange happened. I was looking at my dog savagely barking, and I looked at the animal. The animal seemed to have no fear of Casey and was not even looking at her; it was looking directly at me. Moreover, I sensed that it was not scared, and also, from its body language, it was not a threat to us. However, having remembered stories of women being abducted by Bigfoot, I told my daughter to jump into the truck, and we quickly left.

On the way home, and for the next hour or so, I had tried to convince myself that the animal's movements were random and not associated with my pointing at it. I imagined that it was a large raven that was swinging around, holding onto a branch with its feet. Or perhaps it was a one-eyed bear going about his business, not making any noise and not bothered by my dog. Later, when we got home, I could not dismiss the timing or the hurried directed motion that the creature made when trying to duck out of sight. The more I thought about it, the more it seemed that the thing must have been a Bigfoot. I mustered the courage and asked my brother Steve if he would like to go and look for a Bigfoot.

Two hours later, my brother and I returned to the site on the Grease Trail. I had my trusty 303 British rifle that I had inherited from my grandfather, and my brother Steve had his 30:06 that he had purchased from another brother of ours. I had told him about the animal watching us, and I pointed out where it was standing. I had left Casey at home as I did not want her to startle it if it was still in the area. I showed him where we had cut the wood, an area he already knew well. We parked my old white truck in the same place and loaded our rifles. We walked over to the area and looked for any tracks or evidence. A trail behind the bush was probably used by all sorts of animals. There were no tracks or obvious hair; however, as we made our way through the trail, it opened up where one could see five large trees, generously distanced from each other. We checked around each tree, but we could not find any footprints as the ground was spongy and covered with several layers of needles and other debris. We were so focused on looking at the minute details we almost missed some evidence. I pointed to the largest spruce tree and asked my brother if he had ever seen any animal scat like that. His look was one of surprise: under the tree in question was a rather small pile of coiled feces. My brother was surprised because we had never seen coiled feces in the forest before (unless it was accompanied by toilet paper). Animal scat does not come coiled, but unfortunately, I did not possess the good sense to package the scat and freeze it for future analysis. Moreover, we had never seen a human-like scat so small. The whole thing was no more than the diameter of a silver dollar and no higher than two inches. It was obvious to us, though; it was a territory marker.

The following year, I returned to the same spot alone with Casey. I began sawing on the same pile of wood, and after five minutes of cutting, Casey began barking hysterically in the direction of the same spruce tree. Although I was unable to see anything this time, Casey's behavior indicated that the Bigfoot may have been around again. Rather than stick around, I thought that I may have disturbed it while it was doing something, so I left to get smokehouse wood somewhere else.

After each encounter that I discuss in this book, I will discuss my impressions of the encounter and what I inferred from it. An interesting observation of this experience was that the Bigfoot only had one eye. In some First Nation stories, Indigenous people have claimed to have witnessed Bigfoot individuals fighting with each other and that they attack the eyes to try to blind each other. It may have been that this particular Bigfoot, which I did conclude was a male, was a mature older male and had been in a previous battle over territory. As I believe he was present the following year, perhaps the creek and surrounding area were his main feeding area. His eye was extremely reflective, suggesting a specialization for nocturnal activities. Also, in both instances, he came after hearing the chainsaw. I assume he was attracted and not scared by the sound. Later, I will discuss other instances when they have been attracted to running chainsaws.

Over the next several years, I began regularly visiting the area and taking friends and family to look for tracks. Often, I would find a fresh branch in the center of the clearing, and I could never find which tree it had been broken off. One day, Marty, a city slicker tech guy and total Skeptic, accompanied me to this site. I first explained to him that we would look for tracks as well as the tops of trees that have been broken off. I explained that sometimes Bigfoot would twist off the tops of trees and leave them in the open field, much like grizzly bears claw trees to advertise their size. I told him that I often could not find the actual tree that had been broken, suggesting that they throw or carry them some distance. As I looked in my usual spots near the cedar trees and on the road leading into the clearing, Marty, in a trembling voice, said, "I'm not sure, Mitch, but these look like two giant footprints." I scoffed to myself, thinking that this guy could not find a track if it slapped him in the face, but I walked over to where he was standing, and sure enough, there was a left and right human-shaped footprint, both measuring 17.5 inches long. Both were perfect footprints and had been made in semi-hard dirt when the area was wet. One print had moose droppings, and both had portions of a fine layer of red moss. I thought, however, that I could make a cast of the prints. As I studied the ground looking for more tracks, Marty had moved off to my right and once again, but now in a more trembling voice, said, "Mitch, I think I found one of those branches you were talking about."

Now I was thinking how the heck is this city boy finding these things when I have looked for years without finding any tracks, much less in conjunction with a branch? I walked over to where he was standing, and as if it was all staged, there was the top three feet of a tree lying in the middle of the clearing. We looked for the tree that came off of within a twenty-meter radius and could not find the tree that it came from. Later on, I found a tree with a branch broken about seven feet up, which I thought was a territory marker. The following picture is at the edge of the clearing and shows a freshly broken branch approximately seven feet off the ground.

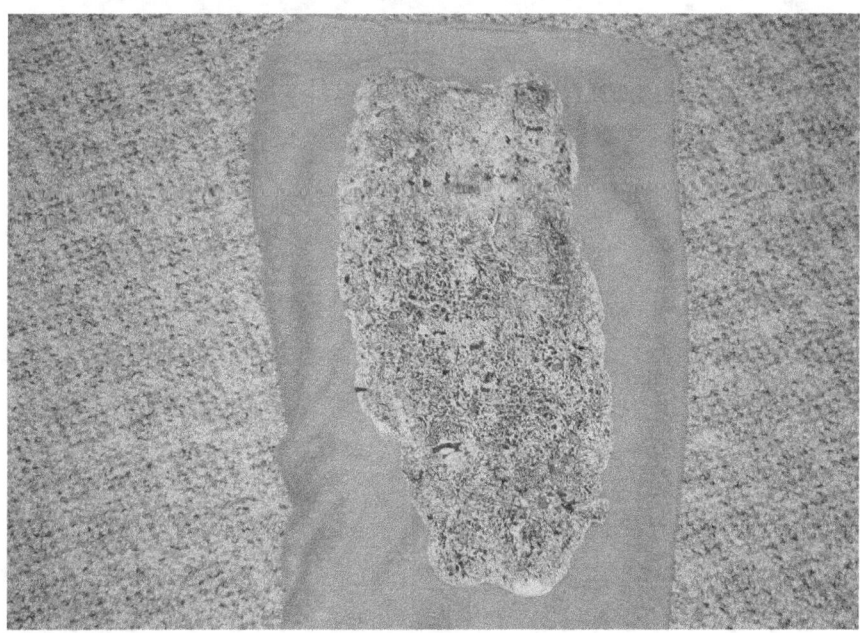

The following day, we returned to the area, and I made one cast of the left footprint. I did not cast both prints for two reasons. First, I did not buy enough plaster, and second, the right print had moose droppings in them, and I am slightly brain-dead. Hence the self-moniker of the "World's Worst Bigfoot Researcher."

Over the next two years, I regularly returned to the site and looked for tracks but found none. In the second year, my wife went to the site to look for a nest of some sort. Initially excited, I found one down the bank and partially dug out under the road, but there was no evidence that any animal was using it as a den. As we walked back to the truck, my wife looked along the bank and said, "What about that thing?" Now I must have walked by or parked near this spot many times but with the leaves in full bloom, there was no way to see it. Now that the leaves had fallen off, a rudimentary bower was evident, as if someone constructed a blind from which to hide. The branches were interwoven with each other, and the length of the entire structure was about eight feet long. Interestingly, it was not a straight bower but one that took almost a 90 degree turn near one end, so it had an L-shaped form. I climbed inside, ran my hand through the detritus, and came up with a fistful of black hair mixed with dead leaves. I went outside the structure, ran my hand through the detritus several times, and came up empty. I climbed inside again, repeating the process. This time I collected the hair and sent it off for a visual analysis, which came back as bear hair. I found a guy on the internet who said he could analyze hair; however, I should have gotten a second opinion. He also claimed one of the hairs was from a racoon, and we don't have racoons in the Nass Valley. Sincethen, the surrounding bush has grown tremendously, and even though it was along a bank just off the road, I haven't been able to find it again. Well, Bigfoot has to sleep somewhere. First, I want to acknowledge all of the people who know that bears can construct simple nests of leaves and sticks and even bend over willows. I have talked to other people who have claimed to have seen what they believed to be Bigfoot nests. In one account, a mushroom picker friend who was picking near the river came upon a strange find. She claimed that they found a constructed frame of willow branches interwoven at the tops of the branches to make a simple roof, much like the one I found. She also said that material had been gathered to provide bedding under simple construction.

The first den I found was below logs that had been stacked so that an old logging road on the Grease Trail could be constructed. It crossed an old creek bed that had flowed to the main creek. A young birch tree grew on the opposite side of the road and down the bank about five feet. It was quite noticeable because it was growing up from the bank, and I took notice of how much it grew each year. My brother-in-law came to visit one year and I took him to the site as he was also a Skeptic. As we neared the site, I was astonished to see that the birch tree was gone. I pulled over and looked over the bank. The birch tree was approximately 12 inches around and had been snapped off approximately five feet off the ground. This was less than 50 meters from where the bower structure was located. I looked around and could not find the snapped-off tree. We got back into the truck and started driving to the bottom of the hill when I saw the birch tree about thirty feet away from the old creek bed. About five feet off the road we found a rudimentary lean-to constructed from the birch tree and approximately twelve evergreens that had also been broken off. They were all leaned up against a small closely clustered group of evergreen trees. One of the trees had clearly been snapped off of a tree standing about twenty feet further into the bush. Eerily, it had been broken off about six to seven feet up. I was able to crawl inside the lean-to and I looked for hair but in this case was unable to find any.

Afterwards, we drove a few meters and parked, and we walked into the clearing so I could show him where the tracks were found and where I had seen the Bigfoot. It had become more grown over, and we tried to walk through some heavy brush to get to the spruce tree. I was able to push back the first few feet of brush, and after stepping into the thick brush, I saw something that I was not expecting. Someone had placed a cement Buddha with a Krishna necklace around its neck. I told my brother-in-law that someone else may have seen the Bigfoot and put the statue there as a spiritual offering. I told him we should break a new trail, but he decided he would take the Buddha statue. I told him not to, but he was adamant. In order to dissuade him, I said that since I found it, it belonged to me, so I took it. Several years later, I made a mulch and ornament garden around a cedar tree in my yard, and that is where the Buddha sits today. If you visit my house, bring some coins to put in his bowl for good luck.

Several years ago, I noticed some private property signs around this area of the Grease Trail, and there was a ribbon across the entrance to the clearing. I also noticed that a road had been cleared and widened across the bridge on the other side of the creek. One Saturday, I decided to drive down the road to meet the new owners and ask permission to put my cameras on their property. As I pulled into their driveway, I noticed they had been working on an old cabin. When I got out of the truck, they were taking a break, sitting around a picnic bench. As I neared them, they looked very surprised to see me. I recognized the guy but not his wife. I asked them what the look of surprise was all about. She said, "we were just talking about you!"

"What about?" I asked.

"Can you make the Bigfoot noises?" she asked.

"Well, they make different sounds but I will make the sounds when they call to each other." So, I made the male and female sounds that they make when they call each other (later on, I'll explain how I know their calling sounds). Their eyes widened. "What?" I asked.

"They were making those calls all day yesterday." I am not sure how they knew me or how they knew what I looked like. The guy was a Nisga'a, and I had seen him around, but I had never met him. I told them some stories about the Bigfoot whose territory their cabin was on and asked them for permission to set up my trail cams across the creek. They were very accommodating and said I could go anywhere on their sixty-acre property to explore for Bigfoot.

Sometime before meeting the couple, someone had told me a story about a guy who had found a rather small human-shaped baby skull covered with dirt and moss. Apparently, he became frightened and put the skull back. After a couple of days, he returned to the spot to retrieve the skull, which was gone. I chalked up that story to probably being a tall tale. However, on one of my visits to the cabin, the property owner started telling me a story when he was looking for deer and moose antlers. He had come to an area near a rock-covered place, not quite open but not quite a deep cave, but cave-like. He had found an antler nearby, and as he passed near the rock-covered semi-cave, he noticed a bump under the dirt. Now, someone might say, "he saw a bump in the ground, and that interested him?" He was also a mushroom picker and bumps in the ground indicate that a mushroom is growing under there. He brushed away the dirt and found a little human-shaped skull. Now he had my attention! He put the skull back, not because he was scared, but because he sensed a spiritual presence in that place, and he was showing respect by putting it back. A couple of days later, he recognized the significance of the find, and he went back to retrieve it. When he got there, the skull was gone. In its place was a moose antler.

5

IT LOOKED LIKE A CHIMPANZEE

Chimpanzees lost off of a train, people who got lost and grew hairy, don't even get me started. These are some stories I have heard to account for Bigfoot in the Nass Valley. When I finished my master's degree program, I relocated to Terrace and began working in Gitlax̱t'aamiks. At that time, there were no available places to rent in the community. After one year, I was able to rent one of the school-district houses. However, when I put in my notice to move from the house in Terrace and was ready to move, the school district called and said the house would not be ready for three months. So, I rented my grandfather's basement. During these three months, I had run into Cyclops on the Grease Trail. Eventually, we were able to move into the school district house. I liked the location as it backed onto a greenbelt, so I could look out at nature every day instead of a road or houses. In the fall of 2000, late August and early September, autumn crept into the Nass Valley a few weeks earlier than usual. Normally warm and sunny until late September, the cool weather came early, and by the end of August, few leaves were remaining on the decid-uous trees. In the forest, the squirrels were digging very deep holes into the base of trees and storing large mounds of conifer seeds. The squirrels were also stripping several varieties of mushrooms and drying the mushroom pieces on tree branches. It was not uncommon to hear of a mushroom picker who had a pine mushroom fall from a tree and bounce off of their head. The cool weather and frantic squirrel behavior indicated that winter might also be making an early appearance.

As the nights grew cool, an air of uneasiness came over the small community. As darkness closed in each night, the dogs in the community became very restless. While the dogs normally began barking when bears entered the community, the barking was limited to a few dogs in that particular area of the community. However, in those few weeks in the fall of 2000, the restlessness of the dogs turned into a maddening cacophony of frantic barking, with the community canines erupting into a seemingly orchestrated symphony of confused throaty warnings mixed with fear. These bouts of frantic barking continued for up to two hours at a time and seemed to wane off in the early hours of the morning. The dogs' strange behavior and the early cool temperatures made me conclude that numerous bears were making nightly trips into all directions into the community. In retrospect, this idea was unrealistic, as bears had no problem ransacking smokehouses and garbage in the daytime. Nevertheless, I had no reason to believe anything else caused the barking.

As I indicated, I had lived on a greenbelt, and every morning, as I drank my coffee, I would look out the dining room window and look for Bigfoot. It became a morning ritual with me, but I had not seen anyone until that one morning. Of course, nothing good lasts forever, and one morning, I was awoken by the noise of heavy equipment. It was earlier than I normally woke up, and I later found out that they were putting in a new road behind the house we were renting to accommodate a new subdivision. The crew started early, and they usually woke me up at about 7:00 am. This went on for over a month, and on one particular day, I awoke and was pleasantly surprised not to hear the equipment. First, concluding that it must be the weekend, I started thinking about what to do for the day. Then I realized that it was not the weekend, and knew I had to get up for work. I got out of bed, took a shower, walked into the kitchen, and started the coffee. It was about 8:00 am, and the sun was shining on a beautiful day. I was looking out my dining window, enjoying my coffee and the beautiful morning view of the somewhat intact greenbelt. I was surprised to see a guy walking along a trail behind several of the neighbors' houses, which ended behind our place.

As I watched this guy walking parallel to the back yards, I knew he was going to become obscured by the conifer trees along the trail that started three houses from mine and that he would come into full view in my back yard. The distance I first saw him was approximately two hundred feet away walking towards my back yard. He looked about five and a half feet tall and was walking slowly with his head down. His hair was medium length and was shiny black, not unusual in a First Nation community. However, I was immediately struck by the fact that his shirt was exactly the same color as his pants, a very dark brown or black color. I was trying to make sense of this scene, and that is when I put two and two together. I concluded that the person was working on the heavy equipment. Hence the equipment was quiet, and also why he was wearing dark-colored coveralls (even though I had never seen that color of coverall before). I knew that in walking towards my house, the person who I now thought was a male mechanic would have to come out of the trail in one of two ways. Either he would change his direction slightly and go off the trail behind the cluster of conifer trees and come out back onto the road that was under construction, or he would come out between my house and my neighbor's house, where there was no fencing. I knew if he came out between our houses, he would have to cut across my backyard to avoid a small swampy area down the bank off my back yard. As I could not tell who he was from his gait, I was curious to see who he was and where he was going.

As he disappeared from view behind a few spruce and hemlock trees, I forgot he was there and began stretching my arms over my head. I saw movement to my left, indicating that he was coming right towards my yard. As I looked over, I saw an arm begin to push down a long, small branch that was crossing the trail at the corner of my yard, and I completely froze, unable to move: the arm that began to push down the chest-high branch was covered with a thick dark coat of three-inch hair. At no time up to this point did I consciously remember acknowledging that I was looking at a Bigfoot's arm. However, there must have been a tremendous fear at a subconscious level. I have been hunting for most of my life and was a relatively experienced mushroom picker. I had been around black bears for most of my life and had also come face to face with grizzly bears in the forest on three occasions. However, during this experience, my mind seemed to be on autopilot, and my conscious self seemed to be just along for the ride, doomed to try to make sense of this unique experience later.

Although my mind was racing during this experience, paradoxically, I was trying to concentrate on a little patch of hair above his wrist, trying to focus on the rest of the arm. At this time, I could hear myself franticly saying over and over again as fast as I could that it was a bear. I repeated this statement numerous times, seeming to reach a rhythmical crescendo, only to have it crash when the hairy arm completed its action, pushing down the branch as he stepped out in full view. When he stepped into full view, my mental defense system went into full threat mode, and I focused on a patch of beige hairless skin on the left side above his waist and started frantically repeating to myself, "it's a moose, it's a moose, it's a moose." Similar to the crashing crescendo of the bear mantra, the moose mantra fell apart as the Bigfoot began moving. Where he was standing, the only good view of him would have been from my window and possibly the two houses to the right. The Bigfoot was directly facing me, and although he seemed to stand there posing for an eternity, upon reflection, he must have only been standing there facing me for a few seconds. Within those seconds, however, my mind was imprinted with what looked like a chimpanzee, only a little taller and standing somewhat straighter. He looked like a teenage human male but hairier. Along his side, under his arms, was covered with much less hair, and you could see his skin on his side was light colored. The little Bigfoot was slightly bow-legged, and his chest looked without hair and had a barrel shape to it, similar to a gorilla. He was well built in his upper body, and he reminded me of a young body builder featured on "That's Incredible" in the eighties. A part of my mind actually said, "It looks like a chimpanzee," and I could immediately feel my body relaxing from its icy noradrenaline grip. However, a second after I began to feel the relaxing sensation, another part of my mind admonished the part that thought it looked like a chimpanzee. That part of my brain exclaimed, "There are no chimpanzees around here," and I was immediately frozen solid again.

The Bigfoot then started moving into a squatting position to face the back yard of my neighbor's house and her tantalizing garden. As my eyes readjusted and I was forced to start looking again, the Bigfoot moved into a squat position beside a stump. As the Bigfoot bent down and started turning, his face came directly into line with my window, and my face, and our eyes met. His eyes grew large and his face had a truly surprised look. Later on, I had nightmares about this, but his face always appeared like a cartoon drawing, which may have been a tactic that my unconscious employed to protect me. Apparently, I was also quite the frightening sight, as the Bigfoot looked and acted as if he had seen a ghost. He was initially quite startled but quickly composed himself and moved with a quick agility that seemed incomplete without the accompanying comical "whoosh" sound heard in many martial arts movies. Caught half way between squatting and standing when he saw me, the creature moved his upper body and head in one quick motion away from me, pivoting at the hip. I was once again trying to purposefully blur my vision, but I watched him turn and go on all fours. He then went onto his stomach and began crawling over the edge of the bank. I did not see him run away; believe me, I was desperately looking through blurred eyes for something running that somehow would resemble a moose. As soon as the Bigfoot was out of my sight, I could immediately move again. Strangely, I felt energized, and called out to my wife that I had seen a moose in the back yard and that now it was gone. I told a few other people that I had seen a moose in my backyard, but I felt a twinge of guilt when I told the story. This was even though I could not remember what happened. My mind began suppressing the event, which had only happened seconds earlier. Although, on the one hand, I thought I had seen something weird, I was unable to remember it and, therefore, was not prepared to accept that the thing that I saw was anything but a moose.

As the next couple of weeks progressed, I began to experience a distressing sporadic mental event when I looked out the dining room window. I would catch myself having a trance-like flashback of this guy in dark clothing walking up the trail behind the houses, but he would never make it to the end. As soon as I would catch myself having the flashback, the memory would disappear. When a flashback would end, it was like I was jumping for floating memory bubbles, each one popping just before I reached it. After approximately two weeks, I was having a flashback in the dining room, and this time, the bubbles did not pop, and I was able to remember the full event and realized why I had such a strange reaction to seeing a moose. I then had some sort of cathartic release like I had been holding my breath for a long time.

In retrospect, I came up with some interesting observations that may or may not contribute to the Bigfoot discussion. My observation of the Bigfoot indicated that it had previously walked this particular stretch of trail. The ease and comfort of his gait and observing that its head was down suggested a visual habituation to the environment. I also had the distinct impression that he knew exactly where he was going. Furthermore, a later sighting in the back-yard and tracks he left suggest that the Bigfoot was familiar with the area and he knew where to hide. The interesting thing is that I believe that this Bigfoot was taught or had learned that he would be camouflaged from view by the line of deciduous trees that lined the path of his route. However, because the leaves had fallen early that year, almost his entire route was exposed. The interesting thing was that he was unable to ascertain this fact, and it provides interesting speculation as to the creature's intelligence. Perhaps the conditioned routine of many trips to the area desensitized him to the presence of his cover, or perhaps he was not at an intellectually sufficient stage of his development to logically determine the principles of camouflage. Actually, had any of my neighbors been looking out their windows, they would have seen him walking up behind the houses.

After accepting that I had seen a Bigfoot, I called my daughter Christina into the computer room and told her I had something to share with her. I imagined that her wonderment and elation would be matched only by my own. However, all she did was look at me seemingly unsurprised, and say, "you should go and talk to mom. She saw a guy with a fur coat run through the back yard a few days ago."

I waited for my wife to get home and asked her about the guy in the fur coat. She said, "it wasn't a guy in a fur coat. Your mother told me to say that. She did not want people to think we were crazy." She had been smoking a cigarette underneath the carport at night, and she had taken Casey out before we went to bed. While she was standing under the edge of the carport straddling the back yard, Casey was pacing back and forth across some unseen but real border between the edge of the carport and the backyard. Casey began frantically barking at a dark area of the backyard, and although she was straining to reach the backyard as if she was pulling on a leash, nothing was holding her back.

My wife was looking into the backyard, straining her eyes to see anything that might indicate danger. As we are very used to bears being in our community, she could not understand why the dog was not going into the backyard and checking out what was there. As a car came down the road, rays from a headlight shone into the backyard, and my wife could see what she claimed to be what looked like a person squatting down in the tall grass in the backyard. When the headlight shone on its arm, she indicated that the person jumped up about seven feet into the air like a monkey and ran away, and with what she claimed to only be a few strides, covered the backyard and into the darkness. She claimed that the guy was not very tall and that several inches of hair were hanging from the under part of his arm. She also indicated that he ran to the same trail I saw the Bigfoot emerge from. She said it was a Bigfoot but that she was not going to be advertising it.

It was more than likely she saw the same Bigfoot that I saw. This suggested that he got over the shock of our encounter well before I did and resumed his usual activities, including hanging out in the area. My wife saw him squatting, suggesting that this type of body positioning is quite common in the creature's habits. The light coloring of its side was similar to my sighting, and she could also discern the longer length of hair hanging from the back of the elbow, which is a consistent hair pattern in other ape species. The height of the jump and the speed at which the Bigfoot moved suggested that the creature was very agile and extremely strong. And perhaps the most notable inference is he may possibly have been addicted to the second-hand smoke from my wife's cigarette because if my wife had her smoking session interrupted, she might have jumped seven feet into the air as well.

Provided with some encouragement of another sighting, I asked one of my uncles, a retired Norwegian ship builder named Martin, if he would look around with me to see if we could find some tracks. Martin is a great guy with some funny stories and a lot of time to tell them. Martin had been in a serious car accident when he was younger and was in a coma for several years. When he awoke in the hospital on New Year's Day several years later, he actually stood up, not realizing he had been in a coma, and tried to walk to the bathroom. A nurse entered the room, completely surprised, and told him that he had been in a coma for three years. Martin later found out that his family's boat and ship building company was gone, and the money had been court-ordered to his ex-wife years earlier. Fortunately for Martin and our family, he met my aunt, and the rest is history.

Martin first thought my wife and my sighting were incredulous, but he decided to humor me. Armed with a camera, off we went to search for clues of the Bigfoot mystery. My 35 mm camera was not working properly, and the film tended to get stuck. I told my uncle we were looking for small footprints, probably the same size as our feet. As I had already looked around the trail where I had seen the Bigfoot and had found nothing, we decided to start moving towards trails that went through the forest below our place. We crossed two roads (the first being the newly constructed road behind our home), and the second road was rarely used as there were no homes along it, leading to the community's sewage lagoons. Below that was the edge of the lava-beds, close to where people had seen Bigfoot in earlier stories I shared. The first interesting thing I noticed was that a medium-sized boulder, approximately fifty pounds, was lying in the ditch on the roadside. I told my uncle that someone must have lifted the boulder out of the bank and thrown it in the ditch. He thought that a grizzly could have done it and tried to explain how their strength allows them to move heavier objects. I agreed that grizzlies were strong; however, they would lack the dexterity to remove the boulder delicately without disturbing any of the surrounding dirt. The hole from the original place of the stone was completely undisturbed around its edges. We decided to test his theory and placed the stone back in its original hole. He positioned himself as a grizzly and tried to remove the stone without disturbing the surrounding dirt. Of course, he was unable to do the task. Grizzlies are very dexterous and could lift a stone directly upwards with both paws, but it would have left some evidence that they scraped or flipped the large rock, and soft dirt surrounding the rock would have left some impression of the bear.

Somewhat energized by this possible evidence site, I stepped off the road, up the bank, and into the long grass. I was immediately struck by a pattern of footsteps in the long grass and quickly called out to my uncle. He looked at the pattern of footsteps approximately four and half feet apart. He suggested that it was nothing and wandered away from me, looking on the other side of a large spruce tree. I continued to look and found a footprint in some elevated dirt that was situated in between grass on either side. The footprint appeared to be thin compared to its length. However, one could not see the toes or heal as they would have landed on the grass. I called my uncle over, and he agreed that it was a footprint and that the footprint was along the line of the footprints in the grass. I took a picture of the footprint; however, the picture did not capture it very well. My estimation of the foot-print would have been approximately sixteen inches long but the middle of the foot was rather slender: only about four to five inches wide.

My uncle walked back over to where he was earlier on the other side of the spruce tree and quickly called out to me that he had found some good tracks. I walked to where he was and found similar foot-prints in the grass. There were more tracks in a row, and he was standing in one print and trying to stretch his other foot towards the other print. Even with him stretching, he would have needed another two feet to reach the next footprint. I quickly pointed out to my uncle that his find looked exactly the same as my find and that his find held no more significance than mine. We razzed each other for a couple of minutes about which set of tracks were better, and then we found some great footprint impressions on softer ground. The Bigfoot must have been walking back and forth through that area because the foot-prints crossed each other.

After taking the pictures, we began making our way back up to the other two roads towards my place. Although we had found some evidence, it was definitely not overwhelming. We continued to search as we made our way back, and I was very frustrated when we reached the skidder trail behind my house. I verbalized a few expletives and told him that we were never going to find anything. I told him we should scour the ground like we were looking for mushroom cracks and bumps in the moss. He agreed, and I looked down beside my shoe and saw a fully formed impression of a right foot. Not surprisingly, the footprint was approximately the same size as mine. I pointed to the footprint and excitedly showed my uncle. He appeared impressed with the find as a wide smile broke out across his face.

The footprint was approximately nine inches long from the big toe to the heel. The arch and heel were not as well defined in the hard skidder trail, only making a quarter-centimeter indentation. However, the front pad and at least four toes were well-defined. In addition, the toes were dug into the ground as if the creature that made them was squatting down. The big toe was dug into the ground approximately three-quarters of an inch. There had been a small yellow leaf where the big toe had pressed into the ground and had formed a nice impression in the toe hole. The next three toes were similar to the big toe in that there was a tendency for a rounded shape rather than an elongated shape. The impression of the baby toe was barely visible, and one had the feeling that it was a very small toe. I tried to photograph the print, but the film jammed in the camera. I went inside, grabbed the Polaroid camera, and took a picture of the footprint with Martin's around the print showing the size.

We were quite happy with the discovery and decided that we were going to get some plaster on the weekend and take some casts. We were so excited that we almost overlooked another print that was beside the footprint; however, it was in the softer dirt beside the skidder trail. Neither my uncle nor I were able to discern what the track was. To me, the track looked like someone had taken some type of metal tool and stamped it into the ground. We both agreed that it looked like some kind of a hand-print. However, the print looked distorted, like the hand was deformed or was a small three-fingered alien hand. Unfortunately, I had only one picture left in the Polaroid camera so I did not get a picture of the alien hand. After I went inside, I looked on the internet for Bigfoot information, and within a few minutes, I realized that the distorted hand print was a knuckle mark left by the squatting Bigfoot. Excited, I met up with my uncle and told him what I thought. A broad smile crept across his face, and he nodded that he agreed. Unfortunately, later that night, it began raining, and it rained for most of the night. I foolishly thought that all of the evidence would have been washed away and did not make an effort to make casts of the tracks. In hindsight, I think that my shock of the experience distorted my perception of my ability to gather proper evidence documenting the event. Either that, or I am the World's Worst Bigfoot Researcher.

I was, however, able to make some interesting observations of the experience.

First, that the toes were rounded as opposed oblong shape. Secondly, the knuckle mark was much larger than one would have expected based on the size of the footprint, the deeper measurement of the toes compared to the arch and heel indicates that the Bigfoot was squatting. In addition, the fact that the Bigfoot print even made an impression was important. The skidder trail was over one year old, and the dirt had been compacted. I was approximately 170 pounds then and did not even make an impression with my shoes on. This may suggest that although this particular Bigfoot was not tall, he may have been densely muscled and possibly weighed over two hundred pounds. Supporting evidence for this indication of dense weight was the deep indentation of the knuckle mark. The mark was fairly deep and suggested that a heavier individual made the mark. Also, the direction of the tracks and trails indicated that those particular Bigfoot were traveling from the direction of the lava bed and were likely the ones based around Vetter Creek.

I had a chance to chat with the village's head administrator a couple of years ago, and I told her I heard some recent Bigfoot encounters. She said she had heard about a couple, but it was nothing like 2010. I lived in Gitlaxt'aamiks for three years and then bought a four-acre house and barn with a creek running through the property, located approximately six kilometers north of Gitlaxt'aamiks. Boy, oh boy, did I move from the frying pan into the fire.

6

LIFE ON TANKERS ROAD

After living in the community of Gitlax̱'taamiks for three years, I found a property in the Nass Valley for sale. It was on Tankers Road, about 6 kilometers north of Gitlax̱'taamiks and 5 south of the Grease Trail. There were four others along Tankers road. The property size was four acres and had a creek running through it. The house had a log bottom and a lumber-framed second floor. The area itself was scenic, quiet, and private. The neighborhood backed onto a high ridge that stretched for kilometers in north and south directions. A large mountain majestically sat behind the ridge, with its center carved by an ancient glacier. The property had an unpainted barn and, while quite old, had a weathered character suggesting both history and utility. When I first went to look at the house and property, I was taken aback. The yard was overgrown with weeds, wild raspberry, and tree saplings in several spots. The house did not have any siding. It had sheathing wrap, but it had been shredded from many years of the unrelenting Nass Valley winds. I found the wife of the couple who owned the house in the back yard spraying a garden hose, so I thought she was watering the lawn. Rather, she had accidentally burnt down their travel trailer, and she was making sure the adjacent forest did not catch fire. All that was left of the travel trailer was a flattened section of steaming melted aluminum and rubber.

I waited until she was satisfied that the fire was out, and we went inside. I first noticed that the hallway leading to the kitchen was very narrow. I asked about it, and she said that you couldn't even fit any appliances through the hallway and needed to use the living room sliding door. A house for Hobbits, I mused to myself, perfect for me and my family. There was no flooring throughout the entire house other than the sub-floors, and the single downstairs bathroom was in dire straights. There was no bath-tub, and the small shower stall was leaning slightly. Part of the bathroom had been framed, and drywall put up. However, a portion still had logs showing. The kitchen had a low ceiling and a ceiling-high cabinet, and the closet was plunked in the middle, which housed the fridge and a broom closet. This meant that the light from the kitchen window could not penetrate the rest of the downstairs, making the first floor rather dark. There were four bedrooms upstairs, and none were finished. The family also had pets, and indications were that the pets had more bathroom space in the home than the people had. Despite all of this, I saw the potential in the property and the house. The yard was huge, and across the creek was a barb-wired space for their horse, which I thought would make a great garden. In addition, the lack of anything in the house gave me a blank canvas to make it our own. Before I left, I made an offer that was less than what they wanted, and eventually, they accepted it. They never did mention anything about Bigfoot.

The day for us to take possession of the house came, and to no surprise, they left their garbage behind. The first job was several trips to the dump. I had not taken my kids to see the property yet, so they were shocked at the state of the house. I had planned to renovate their bedrooms first, so they would feel more comfortable there. We stopped at the bathroom when I was taking them on a tour as first-time home owners. There was a general all-round look of disbelief. We then stepped into the kitchen. I jokingly said the house had good bones as I pulled on the sink and counter. The sink and counter bowed out toward me about three inches, something I was not expecting and something my kids thought was hilarious. I poked at the drywall (the irony) behind the counter, and my finger almost went through: it was completely saturated with water. I immediately hired some guys to start renovating the kitchen and bathroom, and I started on the bedrooms. A friend and I widened the hall-way, and the renovations didn't stop for five years. However, this book is not about my adventure into rural renovations. It is about Bigfoot and our property.

We did not have livestock, and I used the barn as a wood-shed and storage area for my power tools and hand tools. The first thing that started happening within the first year of living there was that I would regularly find my axe or sledgehammer in the back yard. Only two of my kids at the time would have been strong enough to move the sledgehammer, and they adamantly claimed that they were not touching the tools. I had no idea what was moving my tools until I read a story online. A woman claimed she had taken her kids camping at a lake. While sitting around the camp-fire, a Bigfoot approached their camp (it had glowing red eyes). The family hastily left, but on the way to the camp-site, they had passed an old cabin on the other side of the lake and decided to hunker down and use the cabin for shelter during the night. A couple of hours later, while her family slept, the mother heard the door to the cabin open, and a very heavy creature stepped inside. She concluded that the Bigfoot had followed them. She was terrified and pretended to be asleep. She claimed that the Bigfoot grabbed her axe, but it did not pick it up like a person would; rather, the Bigfoot dragged the head of the axe across the floor. It did not stay long, dropped the handle of the axe, and left.

After reading this story, I wondered whether a Bigfoot was going into my barn dragging my hand tools into the backyard and dropping them. I had checked the handles of my hand tools and found no bite marks indicating that a large carnivore had not been dragging my tools around using its jaws. Still, at this point, I had not heard about any Bigfoot in the area, but that was about to change. Kate and Rick moved across the road from me. They were great neighbors, and I also worked with Kate. Kate had some issues with insomnia and was having a rather long bout of it one time. She came to see me at work one day and asked me if I had heard the Bigfoot. I had no clue what she was talking about. She said that she was outside on her deck at 3:00 am the previous night, and could hear a Bigfoot loudly bellowing from the top of the big ridge behind Tankers Road. I thought that because she had been having trouble sleeping for the past few days, perhaps she had been confused about what she heard (I was guilty of assuming, jumping to conclusions, and disqualifying the positive).

As chance would have it, I awoke at 3:00 am that night to use the bathroom. By now, we'd added a en suite. I felt kind of sheepish about it but decided to open the window and have a listen. I immediately heard a sound that Kate's description did not do justice; extremely loud and deep, coming from atop the ridge slightly north of my house. It was being directed south toward the forest above Gitlaxt'aamiks. I had never heard, and have not heard since, anything that bellowed so loud. It was kind of like Arnold Schwarzenegger's roar in "*Predator*" when he challenges the Predator while holding a torch, except multiplied by ten. While it would have been at least a kilometer away, whatever it sounded like was much nearer. My closest neighbor's property is towards the ridge, and I have heard people yelling on their property. In comparison, the yelling was a whisper compared to this, which was much farther away. Interestingly, it clearly sounded like a male, each bellow lasting about twenty seconds and abruptly ending rather than fading out. Between bellows, there was about a one-minute break. I listened to three bellows and went back to bed because I had work in the morning. I did, however, conclude that he was calling to another Bigfoot. I knew by now that the young Bigfoot I saw in Gitlaxt'aamiks had come from Vetter Creek, so I wondered who he was bellowing to. I did entertain the idea he was calling for a mate, which would have meant he was a bachelor. Kate later told me that he had bellowed for a week, and always between the hours of 1:00 am to 3:00 am. I later listened to a cell phone recording taken above Gitlaxt'aamiks, sounding like a Bigfoot was screaming at him. Maybe that's who he was bellowing to.

After that event, I left my bedroom window open from spring to fall to see if I could hear any odd sounds outside my house. A couple of years after the bellowing, I began hearing trees knocking from behind my house. The knocks were always made by two individuals with some distance between them, but the knocks were always close to my property, and they were always fairly close to each other. I assumed that he had found a mate. I had bought a travel trailer we used for camping and parked it in the back yard when we were not using it for camping. I enjoyed sleeping in the camper when it was parked, especially when it was raining. One night, I was in the camper and sleeping on my back. I awoke and sat up in one swift motion, which was definitely not normal for me. A few seconds later, I heard this call from the bush that borders my backyard about thirty feet away. It was a three-octave cooing call, and each successive part of the call was higher than the part before. The call was smooth and sounded like it was coming from a musical instrument rather than an animal. It was a beautiful call, and it was close, too. I quickly concluded it was coming from a female Bigfoot because its voice sounded like it was female. I listened to three calls, each with about a thirty-second break in-between. I describe them as calls because I had the distinct impression it was calling to another Bigfoot, and obviously the male. That realization made me freeze in fear. If it was calling towards its mate, then he was near the trailer. Furthermore, I realized that I had not locked the trailer door, nor had I any protection in the trailer. I had recently started working as a college professor, and the campus where I taught was a three-and-a-half-hour drive away. I looked at the clock and it was around 3:00 am. I lay there terrified and unmoving until the sun came up. I went inside the house, gathered my wits, and left at 9:00 am to work.

Some people may have been dissuaded from sleeping in their travel trailer after an episode like the one I had, but not me. My wife often slept in there with me, but I always locked the door after the episode and, for a time, kept a rifle near the door. One night, I was awoken again by something. It was around 1:00 am. The call that I heard was similar but different from the calls I had heard before. It was a monotone cooing call and was similar to the lowest octave of the female call. The call also ended with a push of air that sounded like a grunt. I knew it was the male calling. It made two calls that night. Later that night, I heard him make the same call. All of his calls were also directed towards my house from the border of mine and my neighbor's property. One night, we were sleeping in the trailer's bedroom; our heads were at the front of the trailer, which was fairly close to the barn's side door. I was awakened by footsteps outside of the front of the trailer. I lifted my head off the pillow, and I'm unsure if it heard me, but it picked up its walking pace. As it moved across the lawn, it sounded like the footsteps that a speedwalker might make. One interesting thing was that it was not walking toward the bushes directly behind my house and backyard. It was walking along the side of the trailer and towards a small section of forest on my property that borders Kitty and Larry's property. I took note of that because I realized that I could set up a trail-camera in that part of the forest. That encounter was too close for comfort, and I finally decided to give up sleeping in the trailer.

I was still pretty new to using trail-cameras, but I did set one up along the trail that went through my little patch of forest leading to Kitty and Larry's property. Animals were clearly using the trail, and not surprisingly, I recorded bears, dogs, squirrels, smaller rodents, ravens, stellar jays, and even my neighbor's horses. I was watching the video-recording one time, and the camera was activated during the night. A couple of seconds later, a large shadow came over the field of light. I placed the cameras at a height of between three and four feet, so whatever made the shadow was tall. The shadow was stationary for about ten seconds, moved slightly in a swaying motion, and then behind the tree the camera was mounted to. That was when I thought Bigfoot was wary of the trail-cams. Although I had set cameras around my property and my neighbor's, I never got clear video of a Bigfoot. Because the hand tools were left in the backyard, the calls came from there, the tree knocking was always from the back, the bellowing was slightly north (to the back of my yard), and the Bigfoot walking past my trailer was moving towards the north, I concluded that they must be coming from a northerly direction. I set up a camera on the post of an old chicken coop about two hundred feet north of my yard on my neighbor's property. I checked my camera one day, and the video showed something strange. My neighbor had dragged the cab of a damaged truck onto his property and left it about ten feet from my camera. He did not notice the camera when he put the truck there. The camera had activated at night, but it had interference on the video for the first couple of seconds as something moved past, but you couldn't see it clearly because of the interference. This camera was six feet off the ground because the grass was high. When the video became clear, there was this truck cab, but inside the cab was two glowing red lights pointed at the camera. Since the truck cab was not there when I set up the camera, I assumed it had reflectors in it, and it only seemed like they were pointing at the camera. I deleted the video (World's Worst Bigfoot Researcher), but when I went to check the truck cab for anything that could reflect two bright red circles, there was nothing. I decided to look around for any tracks, and lo and behold, I found both a footprint and another weird-looking left-sided track that I thought was a footprint with a strange-looking long straight toe. I took pictures of them, took my cousin over, and showed him the tracks.

I went to visit my neighbor to tell them that I found a footprint and a handprint on their property. My neighbor Larry, although claiming to have seen a family of Bigfoot in Alberta and a single Bigfoot standing in a creek about 60 kilometers from our properties, tended to roll his eyes when I told him about the Bigfoot coming around my property. The reality is, to get to my house, the Bigfoot had to cross their property. On this particular day, his wife said that something had been banging on the outside of their house when she had gone to bed over the past few nights. I said I would look around and within a couple of minutes I asked them if they were walking barefoot on their driveway. When they answered no, I asked them to come over, and I showed them an eight-inch footprint near the end of their driveway. The mystery of the wall banger was solved, and now I knew that the Bigfoot couple had two adolescent children.

One of my other neighbors, Gary, manages the highway crew. He told me once that up the highway about 100 meters to the north, he was driving along the power lines between the highway and some forest. He claimed that a Bigfoot ran from the strip of forest nearest the highway, under the power lines, and across the road in front of him into the heavy forest. When I started talking to local people about Bigfoot, I heard that my neighbors, who lived at the end of Tankers Road, had their pictures taken in what they claimed was a Bigfoot nest. As the story went, an area a few kilometers to the north was getting logged. The loggers found a large hemlock tree with a significantly sized structure around the base of the entire tree. As the story went, the loggers left the tree standing with the nest intact. Someone brought my neighbors to the place, and the wife and her friend had their pictures taken standing inside of it. Supposedly, it was four feet high. I asked my neighbor Norm about it once, and he did not even respond. A few weeks ago, I was at the public library in the nearest city and told the librarian that I would start working on my Bigfoot book again. She said that she had a friend who lived in the Nass Valley, and they had seen a large Bigfoot nest. I chuckled and asked if it was Gary or Norm. She looked surprised and said it was Norm. However, she described the nest as a structure that a bower bird would make, which was different from what I originally heard. When I catch up with Norm, I will ask him again.

The only other residential road (it has four houses) in that part of the Nass is a couple of hundred meters north of Tankers Road and is called Irene Meadows Road. Bert Speezak lives at the end of Irene Meadows Road. He has been living in the area for decades. He was visiting Linda and Larry, the neighbors who bought Kate and Rick's property several years back. I came over for a visit while he was there. He said he was walking in the forest behind his property a couple days earlier and must have gotten too close to a female Bigfoot, and she started screaming at him. He left the area immediately and went home. Interestingly, he was a logger and had logged his own property and some areas near his property. Perhaps he was the person who showed Norm and his wife the Bigfoot nest. I will have to ask them.

Across Irene Meadows Road from Bert and across the creek that runs through most of the area properties lived Herb Hewen. Herb was the guy who saved my dog from the wolves a few years earlier. Herb was around 69 years old and continued to work a trap line in the area. Herb lived like he was in the old days, and his house had no electricity. He had lived in the area since he was a small child, and his family was one of the original homesteaders. I ran into Herb and asked him if he wanted to come over for dinner. Before he came over, I had worked the day teaching in Smithers. I decided to come home on the back route to the Nass, which meant I had to take a right turn on the highway at the Gitwanga Junction and travel 82 kilometers until I arrived at the Nass Forest Service Road, which led to the Nisga'a villages. I passed the highway sign indicating where the Nass Valley began, and dusk was setting in. As I was driving, I noticed something crossing the road from a swamp on one side of the highway to a swamp on the other side. As I got closer to it, I was pretty shocked: it was a turtle. I was shocked because turtles do not live in the Nass, or so I thought.

The next evening, Herb came over, and we ate dinner. Afterwards, I asked him about his Bigfoot experiences, as I had heard he knew something about them. He told me that when he was a boy, they gathered firewood every weekend during the winter. They traveled with a couple of horses and a horse sleigh. Each weekend, they would follow their old trail, but alongside their trail would be a trail of Bigfoot tracks, and all of the horse dung would be gone. I asked him what he thought about that, and he figured the Bigfoot was taking the dung and bringing it back to where they lived to eat. This made some sense to me as horse dung still has a lot of nutrients because of the inefficiency of the horse gut in extracting all the nutrients from its food. In the summer, he said a Bigfoot would come to their homestead and dig through his mother's compost pile. It left tracks around the pile, and once he said the Bigfoot must have slipped and fallen down a small bank above the compost pile because it had left slip marks, and they could see where the Bigfoot landed on its butt. After we shared some Bigfoot stories, he told me about a small venomous white snake living in the Nass Valley, concentrated near the river off the Grease Trail. He said that a Nisga'a elder from Old Aiyansh showed him where they nested in the winter and swam in the back eddies of the Nass River. He said that the snakes were extremely fast, but he had caught a couple of them, splayed them on planks of wood, and brought them to Terrace to the conservation office, but they never contacted him back. Herb said that the snakes reminded him of a Scottish adder. Funny enough, I was at a mushroom shack a couple of years earlier, and two Aboriginal fellows from southern BC had come to the Nass for the first time to pick mushrooms. One of them said that he had popped a mushroom out of the moss earlier that day and a small white snake slithered out of the hole and quickly moved across it. Well, everyone in the mushroom shack erupted in laughter. He asked us what was so funny, and we told him there are no snakes like that in the Nass. Since they were new to the Nass, and I liked these guys, I advised them to pick mushrooms and stay safe since they were picking on the Grease Trail, and it was easy to get lost there. I said to them, "If it's starting to get dark and you're lost, do not try to find your way out in the dark. Find a tree with large branches to keep you dry and make a fire to keep you warm. When it gets dark, first, the grizzlies will come. Soon after, Bigfoot will show up, and the grizzlies will leave. The Bigfoot will stay with you until the dawn comes. They will be there to watch over you. When daylight comes, you will have a renewed perspective and then move toward the sunrise and find the road. I will pick up the story of these two visitors later in the book and explain the foundation of my advice to them.

After Herb shared his story about the snakes, he said I would never guess what kind of animal lives in the Nass. I felt this weird feeling come over me, and I said, "Don't say turtles." As I said the word turtles, he said the word turtles at the same time, and we both looked at each other with wide eyes, and began laughing. I told him about the turtle I saw the day before. He told me that when he was a kid, another kid showed him some grizzly bear wallowing holes that were always filled with water back then: nowadays, they are mostly dry. His friend reached into a wallowing hole and pulled up a turtle. Herb tried another hole, and he pulled up a turtle. His friend said that there were turtles in all of the holes. I liked Herb and his interesting stories of wildlife in the area. Herb passed away eight years ago, the same year as Casey did. I miss them both.

One morning in late spring, Martha and Gary (manager of the highways crew) had put their horses out in the field behind my house. This was the year after Herb told me about the Bigfoot collecting horse dung. They had placed their horses in a spot bordered by the bush at the edge of my yard, so I was concerned that a Bigfoot might move through the bush to check out the horses and maybe, you know, grab some dung. When I came home that night from Smithers, my daughter Maria said that my son Nathan had seen something in the bush earlier in the day after school. I asked Nathan what happened. He said that he was shooting the hockey ball at the net on the driveway, and he missed the net. When he went to grab the ball, he saw some movement in the bush across the yard and looked over. He said that he saw a very tall, very large black animal walking through the bush to the edge where the horses were, and then it squatted down and began watching the horses. I asked him if it was a big bear, and he snapped at me and said it was a Bigfoot.

So, at this point, I had more than enough evidence over at least eight years that the Bigfoot came from a northern direction. So, I began taking trips up the highway and driving down the logging roads off to the right, looking for any sign that might indicate Bigfoot were around. Over the next few months, I had checked several roads but had not seen any evidence. There was a final road off to the right just before Nass Camp and just before you started driving on the Nass Forest Service Road. I drove down a section about a kilometer long, and then the area opened up into an old logging area. Something stood out like a sore thumb. Part way up a big ridge extending a half kilometer to the south and continued past eye-sight range to the north, was a huge boulder balanced on a short skinny stump. In addition, a clear trail came down from the ridge towards the boulder. The tracks on the trail were obvious, but what was interesting was that the tracks at certain places moved behind a tree. I believed that this was an obvious Bigfoot territory marker. Later, I found out that a miner in the old days had written a book about the Nass and indicated that up in the mountain behind this particular ridge hill, he found a cave that he believed Bigfoot lived in. I had, and have continued to visit this place to look for Bigfoot. The Bigfoot Road, as I call it, ends after about a kilometer and a half but winds around a bit. One time, I was driving along around a bend, and there were about ten boulders scattered across the road. More oddly, it was at a spot on the road with a trail into the bush. When I first started driving on that road, I had seen the trail, but it was always overgrown and a bit spooky. This was odd because I am not one to be spooked by the forest. I moved the boulders off to the side of the road. In the second to last chapter, I will discuss boulders on the road and another Bigfoot researcher I had met in Prince George six years ago.

Seven years ago, I returned to the Nass for the summer after finishing my first year of courses for my PhD program. My wife at the time had some family visiting, and we all decided to go out and get a few loads of firewood. There were three ladies in the van, and Guy-Guy (yes, that's his name) and I were in the pickup. We nearly filled the pickup when we drove along Bigfoot Road. It was late spring/early summer, but we saw a long pine tree hidden among the fireweed. We had already been to the end of Bigfoot Road and had turned around, so the truck was parked on a slight down-hill slope, and the van was parked about fifteen feet down the slope in front of us. Before we began to chainsaw the tree, I told him this was one of my Bigfoot research areas. He looked at me like I was crazy. The pine tree was long and thick, so we had only sawed about half of it, and the truck was full. There was still about 20-25 feet of visible log left (I could not see the back portion of the log as the fireweed obscured it), which I was going to come and get at a later date. Guy-Guy and I shut off our saws and put them on the ground. We noticed that the ladies were all excitedly looking up at the same hill where the big rock had once been balanced on the stump, but the spot they were looking at was much higher up and about three hundred meters to the south of the rock on the stump. We walked over and asked what was going on. They all pointed up to a spot where the bare section of the hill met the forest edge and said they saw a black animal walking upright, and then it ran into the forest. Guy-Guy looked at me, surprised, and I think he gulped. We walked over to the truck and put our saws into the back of the pickup onto the stacked firewood. What happened next made my blood run cold.

We heard an extremely loud thunderous crack beside us, and although seemingly a cliché, we both jumped a few inches off the ground. We looked over to our left, and the end of the log we had finished cutting started lifting off the ground. I could not believe my eyes as it slowly rose into the air. It was like I was dreaming; if you can say something was surreal, this was it. As the end of the tree continued to rise, I realized that something must have been putting pressure on the other end of the tree to make the end nearest us go up. Moreover, the tree was facing downhill, so whatever was putting the pressure on the other end must have been immensely strong, as I estimated the remainder of the log to have weighed at least 700 to 1000 pounds. I looked at where I thought the other end of the tree would be, but I could not see anything moving, including the fireweed. Finally, the tree stopped rising at about a 50 to 60-degree angle about ten feet above the ground. Guy-Guy and I looked at each other, and we did not have to say anything; neither did the ladies. We all quickly jumped into the vehicles and started driving home. However, as we slowly drove away, I had several thoughts like this. "These are the Bigfoot who come to my neighborhood. I think we just got in between the male and female: her on the hill and him pushing or pulling on the log. He knows what my truck looks like, he knows it's me, and he knows where I live. What would I do if I was him?" The answer was chilling, "Well, I would go down to my house tonight or tomorrow and let me know that he knows it was me and knows where I live."

The next morning, the relatives left. That evening, around 9:00 pm, Nathan and I were bucking up a large birch tree we had fallen a few days before. We were in our yard beside my patch of forest that borders Kitty and Larry's property, and I was telling Nathan what had happened the day before on the Bigfoot Road. I had just finished telling him that I was predicting that the male Bigfoot was coming over to caution me about getting in between him and his mate when I had the distinct and strong impression that something was watching us. I told Nathan I thought the big male had arrived and was watching us. This feeling that I had was unique to me. It was as if I knew he was there. It wasn't just that he was there, but that he was there watching, letting me know. I walked a few feet to where the edge of my lawn meets the patch of forest between mine and Kitty and Larry's property and visually scanned the area. The year before, Larry had cut down all the trees on his side of the property boundary so I could now see daylight through the trees on my side. There was only one small area, and unfortunately, the closest part of the forest patch to us, that was obscured by a few trees grouped ,resulting in a shadowed area. I tried to look for any movement or physical form, but I did not see anything. All of a sudden, my Rottweiler Milo jumped to his feet. He raised his head and looked over at exactly the same spot I was looking. He lazily began walking over to the area, but as his right foot crossed over from the lawn to the forest floor, we heard a loud knock on one of the trees in the shadows. As his left foot crossed the edge of the lawn, we heard two loud knocks from the same spot in extremely quick succession. Milo did not look alarmed and calmly stopped and turned around like nothing happened; that was odd. I told Nathan to get into the house. For the most part, I do not think that this particular Bigfoot was a threat to us. However, I learned from this experience that they do not like it when you get in-between them. Also, because I had predicted what he would do based on what I thought I would do in a similar circumstance, I was starting to think that these creatures had thought processes similar to those of humans.

Three years ago, my girlfriend and I drove along the Bigfoot Road early in the spring, and the entrance to a trail was open and not over-grown. I tried to coax her up the trail, but my Bigfoot stories unnerved her even though she claimed not to believe in Bigfoot. I walked approximately fifteen steps into the trail, where it winded up a small hill, and I saw one fresh track in the moss. The footprint was made by a heavy Bigfoot as the footprint was sunken in and heavy enough to press the moss into the darker duff underneath. The print was 17.5 inches long, but wasn't as wide as I expected. Now, I had a good place to set up my trail cams.

This place was a goldmine for animal videos. Almost every time I changed the video card, I had a great video of black bears, grizzly bears, deer, moose, lynx, bobcats, martins, wolves, coyotes, and birds. By this point, I had been putting out trail-cams for at least twelve years, mainly on the Grease Trail and around our local properties. My first trail cams were powered by D batteries, and the light that came on at night was the same as a flashlight. My later trail-cams had infrared lights and motion sensors. My most recent trail-cams were also infrared but did not show indicator lights, and they had heat sensors. My latest trail-cam was high-definition and recorded sound as well. The reason that I bought the high-definition camera with sound was that I captured something on camera that I did not recognize. I will show the still pictures in a later chapter to keep you in suspense. If I talk about the video and show you the pictures now, it won't make sense, so before I show them, I will return to experiences around my property with the Bigfoot family.

After I returned home for the summer, my wife told me that something strange had happened the weekend after I left to start my PhD program. She said that something was in the bush behind the backyard, and it had been crying for three nights in a row but had not cried in the daytime. My daughter Maria said she was in bed one night and heard Milo barking frantically outside near her bedroom. At the same time, she heard something banging quickly on the balcony posts. She said the barking and banging on the post lasted about two minutes. I told her that Milo probably surprised a Bigfoot that was looking in the living room windows. It would also account for why Milo was not too concerned about the Bigfoot banging on the tree in the patch of forest: Milo already had experience with these creatures banging on things.

As I indicated, most Bigfoot noises we hear are at night. My wife and I separated around nine years ago, and I moved back to my property about seven years ago after finishing my courses and working for a year in Prince George. I had a new girlfriend by then, and she came back with me. One morning, I was looking out my bedroom window, and I had an eerie feeling that there was a Bigfoot out there. I carefully looked around the yard and stopped at the willow tree that grew beside the creek. The grass was long there and could easily hide a big animal. I did not see anything and laid back down in bed. Within a few seconds, I heard something running from the direction of the willow tree, past my house and below my bedroom window. It was running on two legs and made a heavy thumping sound when it was running. More interestingly, it must have been carrying something like a tin panel for a roof because you could hear the panel flexing back and forth as the Bigfoot ran with it. I got up and looked across the field at a small shed that wasn't being used anymore. Sure enough, one of the tin panels on the roof was missing.

One night, at around midnight, I heard one of the Bigfoot knocking on a tree behind my property and on Martha and Gary's property beside the creek. There are no trees along the other side of the creek on Kitty and Larry's property, so I knew the knocking was coming from Martha and Gary's property. However, I heard another knock on Kitty and Larry's property directly behind my backyard. We then heard another knock from across the creek and another knock from behind my house, but both knocks were louder this time. Then another louder knock across the creek, and then another louder knock from behind my house, but this time he had hit the tree so hard that you could hear the piece of wood it was using shatter across the tree. This exchange of knocks was different from others I had heard, and there was some sense of urgency to them. Then, we heard a vocalization, which is how I knew the one who broke his club was a male. A couple of seconds after he broke his club, the Bigfoot across the creek screamed much more loudly than a person could. The scream came from directly across the creek. After about five seconds, she screamed the same scream again, but much lower this time. What was so amazing was that she was screaming some type of words. I distinctly had the impression that she was screaming, "get the %$#@ away from me." I know that might be construed as anthropomorphizing, but that was my impression. I told my girlfriend Marie that a bear must have gotten in-between the male and his mate. As soon as daylight came, I got up and walked to the part of the field where I figured the bear must have been, and sure enough, there was a fresh bear track. Not surprisingly, the tracks stopped, and it had moved away from the direction of my house.

Now, I do not want to gloss over the fact that the female Bigfoot seemed to be screaming words. I had an earlier experience with my girlfriend about twenty kilometers from my house. We had driven past Dragon Lake, found an old decommissioned logging road, and figured, yup, better drive up that. We didn't get very far when we came to a wash out where the road was impassible. Water from a beaver dam had washed out the road, and the soft sediment at the bottom did not look safe to cross. We parked the truck, got out, and started looking around. We were about to leave when we heard some branches break on the other side of the beaver dam. I told my girl-friend there was probably a moose over there and to keep quiet. On the other side of the beaver dam was a steep hill that was wooded but I couldn't see how heavily wooded as it was obscured by dense brush that was rather high. After a few seconds, I heard what we thought was a moose moving through the forest in a southern direction. Then, we heard another large animal moving in the opposite direc-tion. Then, they both stopped at the same time. Now, I was a bit perplexed, so we waited. Suddenly, they began running towards each other, passed each other, and stopped at the same time. All the while they were running past each other, they were breaking branches rather emphatically. They would stop for about a minute and then start running past each other again, breaking branches. You could hear they were breaking branches on the trees fairly high up. After a few go-arounds of this, they stopped after each running episode, sounded like they were squatting down, and began making a deep cooing sound to each other, just like I heard when I was in my travel trailer. I whispered to my girlfriend that it was two Bigfoot. They repeated this several times over a ten-minute period. I tried to esti-mate the time it would take them to cross the beaver dam because they behaved as if they did not want us there compared to the time it would take for us to get into the truck. After about fifteen minutes of listening to them, I told her I thought we were upsetting them and should leave. Just then, the one to our left walked over to the other one and said what sounded like three words to him. His voice was deep, and his words were purposeful although I could not under-stand the language. I had the distinct impression he was saying the equivalence of "We should go." Then the other spoke two words, and interestingly, his voice was nearly identical to the first one who spoke.

I know I am anthropomorphizing, but my distinct impression was the second one was agreeing. They both turned away from us, still obscured by the heavy brush and forest and began walking up the steep foresting hill away from us. They were still talking to each other as they walked up the forested hill. We left rather quickly, too, but vowed to return when the water level lowered during the summer months.

Three months later, we returned, and we were able to walk through the water on the washed-out road. We bush-wacked a trail from the road alongside the beaver dam and stopped where the sounds came from. We were surprised by an enormous footprint in the wet mud at the edge of the beaver dam. However, there were tracks of numerous wildlife species, and the huge track did not show any toes as that part of the foot had been pressed onto a small patch of dry grass growing out of the mud. What was surprising was that behind the initial wall of willow and other bushes were two very wide side-by-side trails. I did not feel safe trying to walk up those trails, and even though I have walked up the road to visit the area on a few occasions, I have not encountered these talking Bigfoot since.

Ok, I digress back to my property. We continued to hear trees knocking at night, mostly during August of each year. There were a couple of years, however, that we had not heard anything. One year, I tried to move out the slider on my travel trailer but the motor had died. I had looked on the internet how to manually move out the slider on that particular trailer. I had been working under the trailer in a certain spot over a two-day period but could not figure out how to do it. The YouTube video on the internet describes a different model of trailer made by the same company. After two days, I had given up. Later that night, we heard some tree knocking from two Bigfoot. What was surprising was that the knocking was coming from across Tankers Road, from Linda and Larry's property. That was the first time I heard them tree knocking on that property in twelve years! In the morning, I decided that I would not let the trailer win, and when I approached the side of the trailer I had been working on, the skull of a wolf had been placed on the exact spot underneath the trailer where I had been laying. I figured that the Bigfoot brought me a gift. I was unsure if it was because I had been bringing fruit and leaving it around the trail off of the Bigfoot Road, or they had looked through the window on my back door and saw a big bull skull hanging on my wall and maybe thought I collected skulls. I recently started a job in the Chilcotins as a community psychologist in Tl'et-inqox, and they have no shortage of Bigfoot stories. One of the nurses had rented a small farmhouse, and she often woke to a new animal skull that was left on her porch.

In the past few years, we have had an owl come around, and he usually stays for two to three weeks at a time. The owl makes a specific call, which it repeats over and over, and its call can definitely get on your nerves. It sits high in a tree at the far end of the field behind my backyard. When I found the footprint and handprint a few years ago and the footprint in Kitty and Larry's driveway, I knew that the Bigfoot couple had at least two adolescent children. I also knew they were being mischievous by scratching and banging on Kitty and Larry's bedroom wall at night. A couple of years after buying our property, I started to lock my doors at night. I was not concerned about humans; I was concerned about Bigfoot. One night two years ago, I had not locked the back door because I was going to let our new dog Willow outside before we turned in for the night. At around 9:00 pm, Willow was lying on the living room floor, and she jumped to her feet in one swift motion. She lifted her head and looked towards the hallway leading to the back door. I immediately walked over to the hallway and the back door was wide open. Someone or something had opened it and did so without making enough noise for me to hear. I looked outside and could not see anything, so I locked it. We went upstairs, and I had grabbed a glass of water from our en-suite bathroom, and I heard the familiar owl call. I remarked to Marie that the owl was back, but something was off about the call. First, there was no repeating pattern. Second, the call came from the thin strip of trees between my property and Martha and Gary's. Third, the call was not coming from high up in a tree, but rather, the call had come from a much lower height. I jumped into bed and we heard the call again. A couple of seconds later, there was a second call, and although it mimicked the same owl call, it made the call in a deep, husky voice. Then came what I could only describe as two Bigfoot kids giggling, but not the way people giggle. Their giggling sounded like a person was contracting the muscles near their throat and pushing air out while flicking their tongue across the bottom of their upper lip. At once, I knew it was two adolescent Bigfoot; one male and one female. The adolescent male made the owl sound again in his husky voice, and they started giggling again. I heard the neighbor's door open, and Martha and Gary came out onto their porch. It was too dark to see anything in the strip of trees, and Gary asked, "what was that?" Marty said that it was something trying to sound like an owl. Then, the adolescent male began huffing like a gorilla, loud, fast, and strong. He was not beating his chest, but I half expected him to. Marty and Gary quickly ran inside. I picked up the phone, called them, and asked them what was happening. She explained that something was near their house, pretending to be owls. I asked her to make the giggling sounds, and she mimicked them very well. She asked me what they were, and I told her it was just the brother and sister adolescent Bigfoot being mischievous. Later that evening, I could hear the young male near the end of the field trying to mimic a different type of owl. Once again, the sound was coming from closer to the ground, and that type of owl did not come around our area. However, I have heard those owls near the Bigfoot Road. After these latter vocalizations, I wasn't sure if he was making a joke earlier in the evening, or if he just was not very good at mimicking owl calls. I described earlier how, a few days ago, he was in the field trying to mimic an owl that does not come around here. It was the same owl call he tried to mimic several years ago, and he is still not good at it! He literally sounds like a big man with a deep voice trying to sound like an owl. He might have been looking for his sister. In the next chapter, I will discuss why I think this. Well, with that said, I have pretty much exhausted the stories of our encounters around my property on Tankers Road. I asked my daughter Maria, a great artist, to make up a sign for me with a snarling Bigfoot and the name Beast Creek so I can stick it on the bank of the creek on my property. She has still not made the sign, but I hope she will. It just so happens that other people have had run-ins with members of this family of Bigfoot: particularly in my local mushroom-picking areas. Here are their stories.

7

THE MUSHROOM PATCH

When I first entered a mushroom patch to learn how to pick mushrooms with my family 25 years ago, I was in awe by the serenity of it all. The forest had so many shades of green, from the moss on the forest floor to the tree-top canopy. I only had two weeks to pick mushrooms that year, and I had been lured by stories that the pine mushrooms had reached a peak price of $500 per pound a few years earlier. I was still in a master's degree program in Prince George so I had to squeeze out what time I could because the picking season occurs during the fall semester. While the beauty of the forest captured me, that was one of the worst mushroom picking seasons ever. Plenty of mushrooms were being infested with fleas, even before they popped out of the ground. I brought my son Justin with me that year; he was only nine years old. The only good mushroom we found was when we got lost, and it was only worth five dollars. However, the next year was better, and my uncle and aunt showed me how to find mushrooms under the dirt and under the moss. They were excellent pickers, and I learned a lot from them. Over the next couple of years, I came to the Nass for a couple of weeks each fall to continue learning how to pick. When I finished my master's program, I came back to the Nass to work but took my vacation time in the fall to pick pine mushrooms. Over time, I had over thirty patches across a two-hundred-kilometer stretch that I would pick. In addition to pine mushrooms, I picked 12 other varieties, mostly for personal consumption. Nowadays, I only pick a few patches. Often, I can walk out of the patch with a sixty-pound load and then go back in to retrieve the sixty pounds I stashed. It is nice when you can make two thousand dollars in a four-hour day of picking mushrooms. Unfortunately, you usually only get one chance at the $2000 dollar day because the price drops by 50% or more after the first big mushroom pop. Furthermore, although the picking season can last almost two months, there are only five flushes in any one patch, which limits the number of big picking days. I love picking mushrooms so much I wrote a song about them. Later, I wrote a poem called "*Ode to the Picker*." I am putting in the poem for your enjoyment.

Ode to the Picker

The mushrooms are poppin, their jobs their' a droppin
At night they're not topping, in our little valley
In the distance a flag, so I run with my bag
I look for the brothers, the hat is their mother

I turd in my drawers, there are three chunks or four
The reason is there, a large grizzly bear
The fleas and the worms, there's no reason to pout
I have twenty patches and one's bound to white out

I can do what I want because I'm my own boss
Out here in the forest, I can sleep on the moss
And if you get lost, the Bigfoot will come
To watch and protect you til up comes the sun
We kick back in the shack, cards, drinks, and lies
The stories start growing, price weight and size
But the price it has dropped, to two bucks a pound
What the heck buyers, quit messin around

All of us pickers, know it's based on a lie
A burger and six pack are all I can buy
The days become short, shrooms moldy with slime
Those are the signs, that I'm clear out of time

In spite of the sadness, we let out a cheer
Because one thing's for sure, there's always next year
My feet are real %$#@ sore
But I'm still having fun
Look at that bump, my sweet number one

When I moved to my property, it was within walking distance of my three favorite mushroom patches. We rarely walked to them because hauling out 60 pounds of mushrooms and walking a couple of kilometers is quite a chore. My favorite spot is about a three-kilometer drive away from my house. Where we usually parked, we could pick directly behind the truck and across the road from the truck before even heading down the logging road to the real patch. One day, my ex-wife and I had parked at our usual spot. She was driving that day, and when I opened the passenger side door to put my boots on, I got a whiff of something rotten. Since we had parked at the same spot the day before, I was a bit confused about the smell because there was no smell the day before. I assumed that a mouse had died and started to decompose overnight, releasing a decomposition smell. In hindsight, it was fortunate that we had picked mushrooms at the spot directly behind the truck the day before, and we saw no need to go to that spot that day. We finished putting on our rain-gear and began walking down the road to the patch. We walked for about five minutes with Casey alongside us when we were leveled by a thick blanket of rotten meat stench that immediately caused me to start gagging. The smell was coming from the forest on our left side, and I immediately yelled "Sasquatch" and grabbed her arm, and we started running back to the truck. When we got back to the truck, we caught our breath, and as if on cue, we both started laughing. I asked if she felt any threat from it, and she replied no. I said neither did I, so we began walking back to the patch again. It was interesting that Casey seemed completely un-phased by it all and had not even barked. I told Penny that whatever it was would likely move to the forest on the other side of the road because that part of the forest extends all the way down to the Nass River while the highway borders the other side. I told her to keep her eye out because it might leave a track. She looked down and said, "like that one."

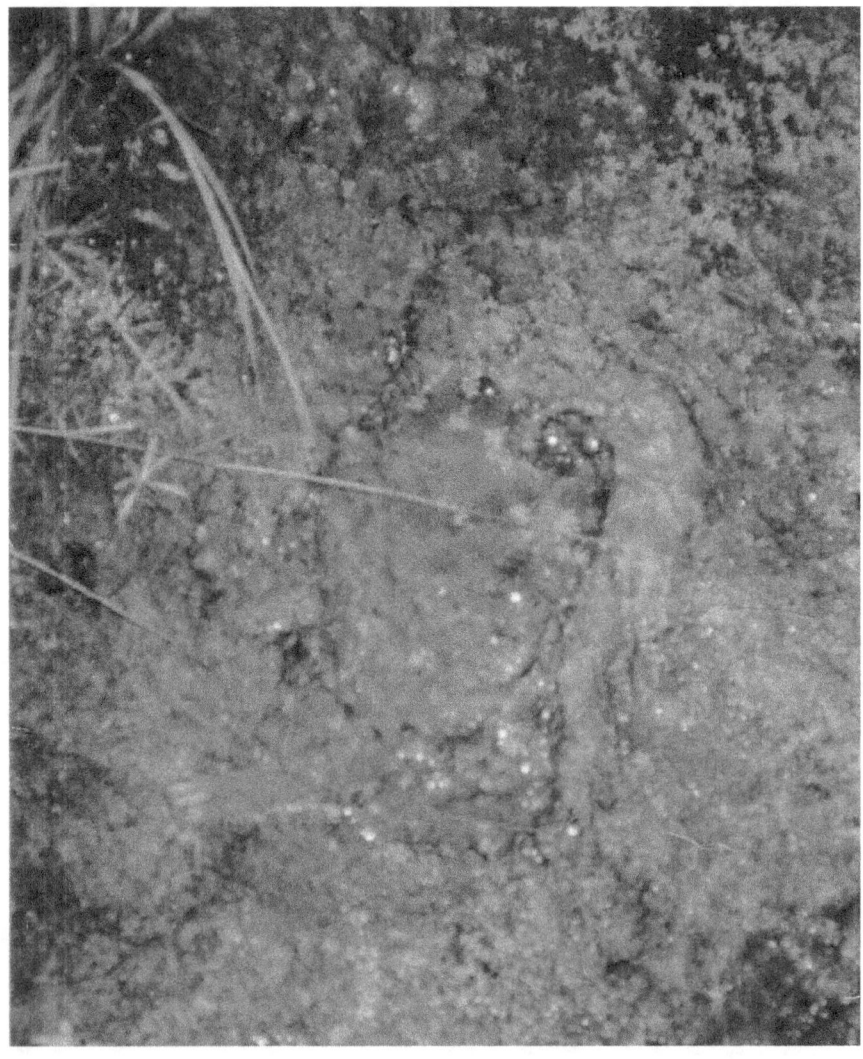

I could not believe my eyes: in the mud on the left side of the road was a large track that was 14.5 inches long and 7.5 inches wide at the heel. Fortunately, we had our camera and took some pictures that day, and over the next several days. An interesting note was that it was a left footprint and no right print. This meant it had stepped onto the road with its left foot and jumped the eight to nine-foot span across the road without leaving a right track. In addition, the one-inch high ridge of mud along-side the track indicated that the Bigfoot was very heavy. The most interesting thing about the footprint was that the foot appeared to have gripped the mud and turned its big toe in like a person would with their thumb.

Although very excited and somewhat apprehensive, we continued our regular picking route. From Casey's frequent barking, it was apparent that the Bigfoot was staying far enough away but may have been following and watching us. Although I had picked this area a hundred times since I had never had another encounter until a couple of years ago, but it wasn't when I was picking. Three years ago, I drove down to the area to scout for firewood and was shocked to see much of it had been logged over the winter. Thank goodness they logged the cedar and left most of the pine and hemlock forest intact. However, when they logged, they left a lot of birch lying all over the place. I had taken a couple of loads out of there, and the next day, I went to grab another load. There was a big puddle near the Y in the road, but I had been sticking to the edge of the road, riding up partly on the bank. For some reason, I decided to try the puddle, and my left tire dropped into a deep hole, leaving my pickup at an odd angle. I could not get my truck out of the hole, so I walked out. I closed the door to the truck and took about five steps when I heard a loud, sharp, throaty whistle behind me directed toward me. It had come from the behind the trees at the Y in the road. I knew it was a Bigfoot, but I just kept walking, and when I was out of sight, I began to jog. I cut across the forest to the river road, and a friend drove by and brought me home. I drove my car to Gitlax̱t'aamiks and found someone to tow me out.

In December 2018, my uncle Herb passed away. At his settlement feast, another uncle of mine, Floyd, asked me to look at a video he had taken on his cell phone. The video was taken in the forest where he was bucking up some firewood, and it showed him panning his camera across the trees. I immediately recognized that part of the forest. While it may seem strange to recognize a part of the forest, parts of the forest look different. The trees are different, the moss is different, the spacing between the trees are different, and the light let into the forest when it is close to a road is completely different compared to when you are deep into the forest. I asked what he was showing me, even though I surmised it had to do something with Bigfoot. He said it was a video of a Bigfoot running through the forest, but it was behind the trees, so you couldn't see it. I told him where he had been getting his wood. He seemed pretty impressed that I knew exactly where he had been and asked how I knew. I told him that I recognized the place and that I had some run-ins with them in that area. I asked how he knew it was a Bigfoot. He said he was sawing up some firewood when he felt that something was watching him. He turned off his saw and turned around, and about five feet behind him stood a Bigfoot. He said he got scared, started his chainsaw, and began waving it toward the Bigfoot. He scared the heck out of the Bigfoot, and it jumped onto a cedar tree only to slide back down. He showed me the video of the cedar tree with long scratch marks on it. Not only did it shred the bark, you could also see that it tore into some of the wood. He then said, "it was as tall as me." I started laughing and said, "was it the boy or the girl?" He looked surprised and said, "the girl." I laughed again and said, "she's just a teenager." And then he exclaimed, "I didn't know that." He then showed a video of a section of the ground and said that she had been sleeping there. That interested me because I wondered why she would be sleeping down in the mushroom patch and not with her family up on Bigfoot Road. I thought maybe she was looking for a mate. I shared my thoughts with my uncle and several other men sitting with us, and I told him that maybe she was checking him out as a suitable mate. We all had a good chuckle over that. The encounter with her, however, took a toll on him. The day after his episode, he was transported by medi-vac to Prince George because of the strain on his heart. I wanted to ask him to take me to the spot where he thought she had been sleeping, but I did not want to stress him. At a later settlement feast, I asked him, and he agreed to show me where she had been sleeping.

One of my favorite picking spots is just across the highway from

Tankers Road. Our family calls it the A to Z patch. I had heard a big animal moving quickly through the bush a few times when I entered the patch, but I had never seen a Bigfoot there. Once, I was walking into the patch and noticed a bunch of branches had been broken off at the height of about ten feet. I walked over to the area and noticed that at the base of where the broken branches were, there were around eight to ten small boulders that were stacked on top of each other. I thought it was a territory marker.

Over the years, I had just assumed that the local family of Bigfoot only came around in late spring to late fall. Other than Herb Hewen, I did not know anyone who said they saw Bigfoot tracks in the snow, not around our area, anyway. In late March 2014, my girlfriend and I decided to take a walk along the power line on the other side of the highway from Tankers Road to look for moose and wolf tracks. We walked along the road and saw some moose and wolf tracks. We walked right into the forest, and I saw a patch of snow where there was no tree canopy. As I took a few steps towards the patch of snow, an impression in the moss off to my right near a tree caught my eye. I walked over to it and to my amazement, there was a left footprint in the moss at the base of a tree, and furthermore, I recognized the footprint. It was the same footprint we photographed of the female Bigfoot; even the big toe was slightly turned inward. She must have been putting all of her weight on her left foot and peeking around the tree at something. Then I realized that she must have been close by because footprints in the thick moss do not remain for too long. I asked my girlfriend to look on the other side of the tree for any more tracks. I stepped over a branch beside the tree and started to look as well. The female Bigfoot must have been watching us because she threw a sizeable chunk of wood through the forest, landing about thirty meters from us. We both jumped, and I told my girlfriend not to move. I told her that the Bigfoot was just trying to distract us so she could make a get-away. After ten minutes of waiting, we left.

Later in the spring, I set up a trail-cam in that part of the forest. As I did, I noticed something interesting. There was a very steep bank along one section of the relatively flat top portion of that mushroom patch. I noticed that there was an animal trail that went up along this steep bank. I followed it part of the way down, and under a large spruce tree, there were two large footprints. They were too large to be the female Bigfoot, so I assumed it was the male. The trail continued down the bank until it reached flat ground and was heading towards the Nass Valley garbage dump, only a kilometer from my place. It was no surprise then when I started hearing stories from the municipal workers at the garbage dump that when they got close to the edge of the dump, something was throwing sticks at them from the forest.

Not only am I lucky to be surrounded by my favorite mushroom patches, Linda and Larry across the road are mushroom buyers. Also, I don't think they believe in Bigfoot, even though all their neighbors do. Several years ago, a mushroom picker was in the A to Z patch. It was starting to get dark, so he came out of the forest and was walking along the side-road heading to the highway and to Linda and Larry's mushroom shack. There was a short-cut to the highway on an open trail, and he began crossing it. He could hear a whole bunch of ravens in the trees squawking up at storm in the forest on his right-hand side. He noted that the behavior of the ravens was odd because the ravens fly from the garbage dump to their territories before it gets dark, and they definitely do not form large groups making a collective racket. Exiting the trail onto the highway, he noticed some movement to his right and looked over. A large Bigfoot walked out of the bush, crossed the highway in front of him, and walked into the forest on my property. The picker ran across the highway down Tankers Road and into Linda and Larry's mushroom shack. He was shaking and out of breath and told the people in the shack what happened. Some believed him, and some did not, but they had all heard the loud clamor of the large group of ravens.

A few years after we moved to our property, I heard a story of a person who had seen a Bigfoot cross the highway near the garbage dump. After getting his number, I called him and asked if he wanted to be interviewed for my book. He was reluctant, and then he just refused. After I had met him a few times, we became friendly, and he asked if I knew it was him who had been driving that evening. I told him that I didn't and asked why he didn't want to talk about it when I phoned him. I realized from his immediate discomfort that he knew about its cultural ramifications. He did tell me about it, though. He said that it was about 8:00 pm, and he saw the Bigfoot walk from the garbage dump side of the highway across the highway and into the forest. Interestingly, the nephew of the women who took the picture of the Bigfoot girl in the gym came and chatted with me and told me that he was in the car with the man. He also told me that two other people were in the car, and all four saw the Bigfoot cross the highway.

Last year, my uncle Marty and I went for a pick at the A to Z patch. Over the past seven years, summer weather began starting in spring, and the rainfall patterns had changed dramatically. Last year was the worst for lack of rainfall. Our area was actually given a level four drought rating. We live in the coastal rainforest, so a level four drought really hit the animals and vegetation hard. There were almost no mushrooms of any kind. As Marty and I moved through the forest, I thought the patch's lower section where the moss tended to stay moist, might produce some mushrooms. We moved down through a small ravine, me in the lead and Marty approximately thirty feet behind me. A smell wafted down the side of the ravine, which I could only describe as the smell of death. I stopped and asked Marty if he could smell anything. He said yes. I told him to get closer to me. I said the smell was coming from something dead, a grizzly bear that had rolled in something dead, or a Bigfoot. I told him we could check on the other side of the bank where the smell was wafting in from but that we needed to be careful in case it was grizzly. We walked through the lower part of the ravine, crossed over, and walked up the hill at the top of the ravine. We could not see nor smell anything atop the hill or on the adjacent hillside. As we walked down the adjacent hillside and got near the bottom, I glanced over my shoulder and saw a white mushroom about sixty feet away. I had lost my glasses the week before when a branch I pushed down sprang back, snagging them and flinging them into a rat's nest of branches somewhere on the ground. Even with a metal detector, we couldn't find them. So, I wasn't sure it was a pine mushroom I had seen, but as

I neared it, I became more convinced it was. I was about ten feet from the mushroom when I heard something move atop the hill we just walked down. I looked up and saw a medium-brown figure standing behind a couple of small trees. He was the same brown color from head to toe, and he had hippie-length hair. He took off running on two feet behind the young trees and down into the ravine we just walked through. I could see it was the height of a regular-sized person, maybe just shy of six feet. He was running very fast, but not like a human. His body was straight up as he ran, and his knees were not coming up high like a person's would. and strangely it looked very straight as it ran. It only had to run about fifteen or twenty feet before disappearing into the ravine. I told Marty I had seen it and there was nothing to worry about. And, oh yeah, it was a pine mushroom.

What was really interesting about seeing the male adolescent Bigfoot was the color of his hair. One year earlier, I went out with my neighbor Larry for a quick pick. We went to the airport patch behind Nass Camp, about seven or eight kilometers from my property. A young fellow was with Larry, so I agreed to stay near the perimeter of the patch with the young guy while Larry walked deeper into the patch. Within a few minutes, we heard Larry yelling at something, which caused me to pull back closer to the road. We then heard him yell, "Grizzly". What I saw next didn't make any sense to me. I saw what looked like a dog boy running on all fours in a weird galloping motion. In that part of the patch, the trees are well spaced apart, so you can see for quite a distance. In addition to how strange he looked and how it moved, it had a strange brown coloring with hair the length of a red setter. Although he was running on all fours, I would have estimated his height at about five foot five to five foot seven. When I saw the bigfoot running down the ravine, I realized it had the same hair color as the dog boy. So, in one year, he had grown a few inches. I told a friend of mine, Cecil, about my experience with the dog boy and how his running on all fours resembled a weird gallop. He then told me that when he was young, he saw a young black Bigfoot running on all fours, and that it reminded him of how a rabbit runs. That struck me as making sense in what I saw at the airport patch. A couple of weeks ago, I came upon a story on the internet regarding a young woman who has trained herself to move and jump like a horse. She has set up her yard with horse jumping bars like they have in dressage. Watch her video if you want to see how a Bigfoot moves on all fours. The main difference is that Bigfoots can move much faster and are far more comfortable in the four-legged gait.

8

THE BIGFOOT ROAD

Some of my experiences over the years did not make much sense to me until I had read people's stories of Bigfoot on the internet or watched Bigfoot stories on TV. On one show I watched, some Bigfoot researchers showed flat rocks on stumps and believed them to be territory markers. However, the rocks were much smaller than the big one I found on the stump. Once, when I was driving down the Bigfoot road, I carefully looked along the road and found a flat rock on a stump that looked remarkably like the one on the TV show.

A few years back, I went to one of the mushroom shacks, and my friends had picked up this guy on the highway who looked like he needed help. His name was Josh, and he had traveled to BC from Nova Scotia. He came to the Nass to pick mushrooms but was woefully unprepared. He did not have the proper footwear, raingear, or tent for our kind of weather. We talked about Bigfoot, and Josh asked us if those animals lived around here. I said yes, and he said when my friends picked him up, he was coming from an area where he had camped the night before and had the get heck out of there. He said that after he made camp, he could hear people running in different directions on either side of his tent. He poked his head out of the tent and yelled at them to leave him alone when he saw one of them stop and look at him, and Josh said it had glowing red eyes. He knew from the size and red eyes that they were not people, but he did not know what they were. I then described to him exactly where he had camped. He was pretty impressed and asked if I had seen his tent set up. I told him I knew where he was camping because he was camping in my Bigfoot research area near the Bigfoot Road. He stayed for the season to pick mushrooms, but he vowed never to go near that area again.

Over the past several years, I have tried different trail-cams, as I have indicated. Part of the problem with using trail-cams in the Nass is the wind. Motion sensor cameras are always going off due to branches and grass being blown around. However, I was still able to get good videos of many animals as I had previously described. One great video I had gotten was from Kitty and Larry's property, not in their field but in the forest on their property. In one video, I caught a black bear running for its life. In a video a minute later, sauntered in a grizzly sow and two second-year cubs. They were thin for grizzlies, and the cubs had very short brown and blonde patches of hair. Two years later, I had my cameras on the trail off Bigfoot Road. Once when I checked my camera, I could see the two cubs however they were now young adults and on their own. The next week, I got video of the young grizzly, and he was alone.

When I first set up a trail camera on this trail, I tied the camera to a tree that directly overlooked the trail. The trail went from the road up a small hill onto a small, relatively flat section and then down a small hill over to a creek. Two years ago, I went to change the video card on the camera and noticed that the camera had been turned off of the trail. It was not turned too much, but it was noticeable. I realized that whatever moved the camera must have approached from the back of the camera as it did not set off the motion sensor. I assumed it must have been a bear. I changed the card and moved the camera back into place. When I looked at the videos, I did not see anything out of the ordinary. The next week I went back to change out the card, and I was pissed off at what I saw. The camera had been twisted around the tree 90 degrees to the right and was pointed at a large stump. I thought a person had done it and that they possibly thought that I was using the camera to scout game for hunting. When I got home to watch the videos, the assumption that a person was responsible changed. As I watched one particular video, I saw the camera move. Then, a few seconds later, I saw a blip across the camera's field of view, which I could not quite understand. I had dozens of animal videos and had never seen anything move that fast. Then, from underneath the camera, a large dark mass of a head was looking directly into the camera. It did not have a snout but was right up against the camera, looking into the lens hole. It rolled over onto one knee, stood up, and walked out of the camera view in one quick motion. Whatever it was, I thought at the time, it was moving abnormally fast. A second after it moved out of the view, the camera turned again all the way around to face the stump. This meant that likely a third Bigfoot finished turning the camera.

When I could go through the video using the super slow-motion setting on my computer, I could see the thing that ran past. It only showed up on one still frame, indicating how fast it was moving. At first, it looked like grey and fog-like, or like flames of a fire. Really, in other circumstances, one might have concluded it was a ghost. I was able to get more still frames of the second animal, which had been lying below the camera. Because its head was so close to the camera, you couldn't really see much. However, you could make out part of its back as it turned. When it stood, you could see its lower butt, hamstring, and part of the calve muscle. You couldn't see its foot. But that first animal bothered me because I couldn't figure out what it was. After three days, I was laying in bed and knew that logically it was a Bigfoot, but the speed of it made the still frame difficult to see. I realized that if it was a Bigfoot, a face should be within the fog-like mass. The next morning, I started changing the video settings on my computer and looking at the video. One particular combination of settings changed the color from grey to bluish, but I could see a face that did not look like what I thought it would be. Rather than looking ape-like, it looked to me to be more dog-like. It had two eyes, and both appeared to be looking downward at the camera. It had a small nose, a bigger mouth, and it appeared to have its tongue hanging out. Once I could make out its face, I could count six human-like teeth. The fire-like flames were actually its hair flowing behind it as it ran. Its hair must have been at least two to three feet long. There was also another interesting thing. Its hair looked like it was neatly parted. That confused me, but I remembered from a primatology course that I took that Bonobos, a chimpanzee species, had a part in the middle of the hair. However, after carefully looking at the picture, it seemed that something was causing the part in the Bigfoot's hair, and you can be the judge, but it looked like a small Bigfoot child sitting on her shoulders. When I showed the video to a guy where I worked, he said that some guys cutting down some trees to make room for a couple of power poles near that area saw that female Bigfoot walking with her small child on her shoulders.

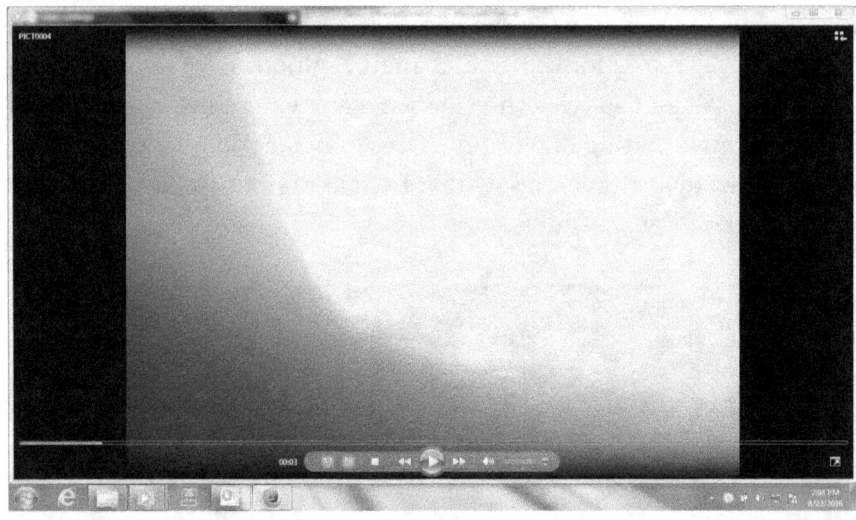

The other parts of the video showing the other Bigfoot were a bit more challenging to interpret because of how close it was to the camera. That was never an issue for my videos before because animals with snouts have at least a few inches of space between the camera and their face, and also, animals do not move fast like these Bigfoot. However, you can see a portion of his back in one still frame. His back is muscular and sparsely haired. It is very similar to a trail-cam video of a Bigfoot's back that you can see on the internet. What is more interesting, however, is the still frame of his leg. While heavily muscled, he appeared to not have any hair on his leg besides a tuft of hair behind his knee.

I had gone to the area with my uncle Marty to change the video cards because I had added an extra camera. After the video of the Bigfoot, who looked like she may have been vocalizing as she ran past the camera, I bought the high-definition camera with sound recording and faced it toward the camera I had recorded the Bigfoot on. We changed the cards and decided to look around on the trail as it headed towards the creek. I got close to the creek, identifying some trees where a camera could be somewhat hidden away from obvious view when I noticed sand along some sections of the creek bank. I told Martin I was going to walk along the creek bed for a short distance, and I was able to see bear tracks imprinted in the black sand. I went along the creek bed for about twenty meters and told Marty I had not found anything and that we should get going. He looked at where I was standing and told me to walk a bit farther and check over a long, thick log that had fallen across the creek bank and into the forest. I stepped over the log, and most of the creek bank was hard rock, but a few feet farther, there was an area with some sand. I walked over and looked, and there were some small bear tracks and some bird tracks. I had to backtrack to cross the log, and as I did, I noticed something on what I thought was just black rock. There was a thin layer of sand alongside the creek, and there was a clear foot-print about 8-9 inches long. More remarkable, however, was that half of an approximate 4-inch track overlapped the bigger track. You could only see the back half of the small track. I went home, grabbed my camera and some flour, and brought my son Nathan back. I put some flour in the track because there was not really any depth to the imprint of the footprints. It was more like a surface imprint or like they had some body oil on their feet that left a film-like shape of their feet. Nathan actually stomped beside their tracks, and he left no physical imprint whatsoever.

9

THE WATCHERS

Ok, now I want to recap how I started on this literary journey and where personal experience had brought me. I'll be brief, but it is necessary because, in these next few chapters, I will describe some stories and personal experiences that have caused me to entertain some outlandish conclusions. Initially skeptical, I saw what I thought was a Bigfoot watching me while hiding around a spruce tree. Later on, we found footprints and what seemed to be Bigfoot structures in the same location. Two years later, I saw a Bigfoot youth in my backyard, and although reluctantly, I had to accept that they were real living creatures. Then, over time, I understood that Bigfoot are not just regular animals. They understand camouflage and purposely communicate through tree knocking, vocalizations, talking, and that they had a sense of humor. Additionally, they brought me a gift (I only say this because I don't know their motive. Perhaps they liked the bananas I had left for them or the wolf skull was meant as a threat). They also have some awareness and caution around trail-cams. The only other animal that I had video-recorded on a trail-cam that was leery of the cameras was a raven. Taken together, all of this suggests that they are highly intelligent.

I had already told several stories in which I had been very close to

Bigfoot and other stories where I was relatively close. In those instances, the people with me and myself easily could have gotten to the Bigfoot, clawed up or pummeled, or whatever. Some stories are told in my culture about Bigfoot fighting each other, and one of their striking tactics is hitting with a closed fist but not with the knuckles but clubbing with the sides of their hands. The point is that even with the opportunity, they did not attack us on those occasions. Moreover, on a couple of those occasions, I perceived that they meant us no harm whatsoever, much in the same way that I might make that conclusion after meeting a person. I have heard stories, such as the one Sim'oogit Bayt Neeklh told of Bigfoot chasing people out of an area, sometime breaking branches and making frightening vocalizations. Given how fast I have seen Bigfoot move, it makes sense that they were only trying to frighten people away and not trying to catch them. Moreover, I had heard a couple of stories suggesting they may even be willing to protect us in certain circumstances.

Quite some years ago, one of my cousins in Laxgalts'ap got lost picking mushrooms on Blueberry Hill. When I was able to talk to her a couple of months later, she told me the most incredible story about her ordeal. Like many mushroom pickers, she decided to leave the forest too late in the evening. Navigating in the dark is not difficult when you know a part of the forest inside and out. However, finding your way out can be difficult when you throw in some tricky terrain, swamps, and devils club patches. On that particular night, although the moon illuminated the forest canopy, my cousin became hopelessly lost. She finally became tired enough that she tried to stop and rest, but then she started to hear the low guttural growls and grunts of a grizzly bear. As you can imagine, she was terrified and began hurriedly moving through the forest. She thought it might be a good idea to run through a large patch of devil's club, hoping the grizzly would not follow her. By this time, clouds must have moved across the moon, and it had gotten very dark, and she could not see anything. However, she could hear the rushing water of the Nass River and thought it was a good idea to make her way towards it and then walk along its bank back towards

Laxgalts'ap. What she did not realize was that she had walked across Blueberry Hill and was atop an adjacent ridge, where a cliff edge was between her and the river. As she was about to take another step, she was startled to hear my grandmother's voice. My grandmother had passed away a couple of years earlier. My cousin heard my grandmother tell her to stop, and my cousin immediately stopped walking...but the river sounded so close. Just then, the clouds moved past the moon and she saw that if she had taken one more step, it would have been over the cliff's edge. Using the moon's light, she backtracked into the forest, walking back on the same trail. As she crossed a log on the trail, she could see the large, fresh print of a grizzly bear. She realized that it had continued to follow her, and she began moving more quickly through the forest. Once again, she found herself off of the trail and smack dab in the middle of a patch of devil's club. Frightened that she was hopelessly lost, she looked down and saw her foot-print facing the other direction. She realized this was the same patch of devil's club he had made her way through earlier. What she saw next made her blood curdle. Alongside her foot-prints was another set of foot-prints. The foot-prints were huge, and they were not grizzly tracks. Now I could not imagine her fear, perceiving that a grizzly, and a Bigfoot were now stalking her. She veered out of the devil's club patch and, after a short period, came to a rocky outcrop. Near the top of the outcrop was a small indentation with a ledge underneath it. She climbed up the rock until she reached the ledge and then crawled into the small indentation. She looked out into the forest abyss as she lay on her side. At the closest edge of the patch of devil's club, she was startled to see two bright red eyes looking at her. As his eyes became accustomed to the darkness and the distance, she saw the figure of a large Bigfoot, which she claimed looked like a giant man. He was leaning against a tree with his left shoulder and just stood there watching her. She was terrified and wondered whether he would be coming to get her. Just then, she heard my grandmother's voice again. My grandmother told her it was a Sasquatch and that it was not there to harm her. Rather, my grandmother told her that the Sasquatch had chased away the grizzly and that he would watch over her until the sun came up.

My cousin was exhausted, and hearing my grandmother's voice greatly relieved her. Although wet and cold, she closed her eyes and fell asleep. While she was asleep, she heard my grandmother's voice again. "Wake up, Mick, wake up." Too exhausted to open her eyes, Mick answered, "No, I can't". Then my grandmother said in a forceful tone, "Wake up, wake up right now." She forced herself to open her eyes and looked out into the forest, but the Bigfoot was gone. She could then hear the sound of an outboard motor and tilted her head towards the sounds. She could see the light from a spotlight shining upwards from the river. Although her muscles were very stiff, she scrambled down the rocky outcropping and approached the light. After a few minutes, she reached the edge of the cliff and waited for a couple of seconds because she needed to gather her strength just to call out. Just before she tried to call for help, the spotlight was on her, and she could hear people on the boat say, "There she is." The men pulled their boat onto the river's bank and made their way up a less steep slope where the cliff wall changed to a forested slope. They had a blanket and hot coffee from a thermos waiting for her. She told me that had they not gotten to her then, she would have succumbed to the hypothermia. She credits her survival to my grandmother's spirit and the Bigfoot that watched over her. Quite a combination.

Earlier in the book, I discussed having met a couple of First Nation guys from Southern BC who came to pick mushrooms in the Nass for the first time. It is quite remarkable how many first-time mushroom pickers I have met who have no sense of the danger related to mushroom picking. Even experienced pickers get lost picking mushrooms; some do not leave the forest alive. Personally, I have had to guide out a number of lost mushroom pickers, some very experienced, and some who even knew the patches well that they had become turned around in. But back to these two young First Nations guys. They had been doing a road pick that day on the Grease Trail. Essentially, they had been parking their vehicle on the side of the road, and picking in the forest within sight of the road. Although it requires years of walking any particular forest patch to truly know where you are at any given time, I am always amazed at the confidence some pickers have about their ability to go farther and farther into the forest without concern for getting lost. Well, after one day of picking the roadside, these two fellas talked about going back the next day and getting deeper into the forest. Naturally, neither had a compass, and even more concerning to me, they had been separating from each other to cover more ground; always a perfect recipe for getting lost. Since I knew the patches on the Grease Trail well, and they described the places along the Trail that they were picking, I advised them on how to safely make it back if one of them got lost. I explained that they could walk over a cliff in the dark if they were to go the wrong way towards the river and not the road. I told them to hunker down and wait for daylight. There is a huge rock cliff to the east that would obscure the morning sun, and if it was cloudy, they would not be able to easily detect the direction of the rising sun, which is the direction of the road. That evening, one of them returned and told us his buddy was lost. The next morning, as we were preparing to go out to look for the lost fellow, they pulled in front of one of the mushroom shacks. Sheepishly, the fellow who had gotten lost stepped out of the car. We were relieved to see him looking no worse for wear. He walked right up to me and thanked me for the advice on how to get out when daylight came. While some of the other guys asked him about why he got lost, his response was predictable: he had begun to find mushrooms and misjudged the time of day, and by the time it began getting dark, everything looked the same. Then, he described how he found a large spruce tree and made a fire to keep warm. Then he exclaimed, "And then Mitch's Bigfoot advice." Everyone chuckled as they knew I was the local Bigfoot guy, but then he went on to tell what happened. After he made the fire, he could hear the sticks on the ground breaking around him. He quickly put more wood on his fire, and as the darkness came over him, at the edges of the illumination from his fire, he could see the four legs of a large grizzly bear slowly walking around him. He was glad he took the time to gather a large number of branches and pieces of wood to fuel his fire. He said that the grizzly continued to walk around in a large circle, occasionally huffing in the chilly night hours. This continued for a few hours when he heard the grizzly quickly move off straight through the forest. A few minutes later he could hear what he thought was the grizzly again, but he was perplexed by the sound of its foot-steps. The foot-steps were louder, and they sounded like two feet rather than four. In addition, there were fewer stick-breaking sounds. As he peered out into the darkness, his firelight shone on two tall and hairy legs, but he could not see the upper portion of the animal. The Bigfoot continued walking around him, roughly the same distance around him that the grizzly had walked. He told us that the Bigfoot stayed with him for the whole night and only walked off as the light from the early morning sun broke through the mist. While we commended him on using his brains to stay safe and that he would be wiser for it, both of them stated that they were packing up and heading south to pick grounds that were more familiar to them. We were disappointed to see them leave.

In both of these stories, Bigfoot came to the aid of lost mushroom pickers while grizzlies were stalking them. Why would a Bigfoot put itself in harm's way to protect vulnerable mushroom pickers from being eaten by a grizzly bear? In addition, the Bigfoot had made itself known to them in both cases. Although I have already indicated my belief that because of my own personal experiences that Bigfoot are very intelligent and human-like in their behavior with each other, the cross-species interactions were very interesting to me. It wasn't until much later, only within the past six years, that I had researched some evidence, heard first-hand accounts of things, and saw some things that I could not explain with even a common reference point among Bigfoot believers.

10

AWARENESS, BELIEF, KNOWLEDGE, AND UNDERSTANDING

T his is the most difficult chapter for me to write. The reason is that over the past eight years, I experienced some Bigfoot phenomena that were downright incomprehensible to me and should be scarcely believable to anyone else. However, these experiences were similar to other peoples' experiences, that when I read or watched videos of their testimonials, I had a hard time believing them. The stories people had told were simply too incredulous. My disbelief was steadfast even though there was linear continuity regarding these types of extraordinary Bigfoot experiences over the past couple of centuries among European settlers and among Indigenous Peoples before that. In this last chapter, I will describe my most challenging experiences with Bigfoot. I will also talk about the most controversial issue surrounding Bigfoot; the conspiracy theory to keep it out of mainstream science.

Indigenous Peoples in North America have told stories about Bigfoot from time immemorial. Interestingly, even the stories among various Indigenous Peoples differ. Some Indigenous groups view Bigfoot as a spirit being that possesses abilities to disappear or can shapeshift into different forms. Some Indigenous groups see Bigfoot as a flesh and blood creature, having the same motivations as other animals to protect its territory from intruding humans. Other Indigenous groups view Bigfoot as being flesh and blood creatures but also having special abilities. Some claim that Bigfoot is a multi-dimensional creature and can move between their own dimension and ours. Interestingly, Indigenous Peoples from Eastern Canada and the central United States tell stories that Bigfoot was brought to earth from the Star People. Essentially, the story goes that the planet where Bigfoot had lived would no longer be habitable, so an alien civilization saved them and brought them to earth. In addition, according to these stories, as a trade-off, Bigfoot was required to watch the people of earth and report back to the Star People. I mean, wow, that is a lot to take in. That was definitely not in my belief system, and in fact, I hadn't heard about these beliefs about Bigfoot being extraterrestrial until the past few years. I guess, however, one of these accounts about Bigfoot must be true. Occams razor suggests that we make the least assumptions, and therefore, we should conclude that Bigfoot are flesh and blood creatures and evolved on earth like the rest of us. However, eyewitness testimony suggests that Bigfoot may possess abilities or technologies that do not align with our understanding of evolution or the progression of technology in primate species on earth.

I think that this will be a bit of a hodge podge chapter, with stories that will require some patience on your part. The Nisga'a have a story called "Spider-Man". Yeah, that is right, Marvel, we had it first. As the story goes, the people in a village moved to the fishing camps for the fishing season. However, one elderly woman stayed behind, and her granddaughter stayed with her. A man came along, dressed in a silver-colored tunic. He was K'amsiiwaa, or the people who have skin the color of bleached wood. He told the grandmother he could make something for them to fish with in the local creek, but he wanted the granddaughter in return. The grandmother agreed, and he began making a gill net out of fireweed and stinging nettle. They tested the net in the creek and were able to catch fish. After a few months, the man told them he had to leave. He explained that the men who dropped him off were coming to pick him up where they had dropped him off. As he walked away, he went behind a large boulder. The granddaughter, who had become fond of him, ran after him, but instead of finding him, she found a large silver spider in the center of a spider web. To her, the spider web resembled the gill net, and the silver color of the spider resembled the silver tunic worn by the man. When the people in the village arrived back, they were surprised to find the smokehouse full of fish. Since then, the Nisga'a have been using gillnets to fish for salmon on the rivers. The Spider Man is known as a Naxnok̲ or spirit being in our culture.

In the Nisga'a culture and many other Indigenous cultures in North America, it is said that the Bigfoot only shows itself to certain people. The reasons for that differ, from those people being worthy of the sighting, being of a pure heart, or possessing abilities that a Shaman might have. Shaman is a Russian word for "one who knows". A simpler explanation would be dumb luck or the increased likelihood of seeing them being correlated with more time spent in the forest compared to people who haven't seen them. Whatever the case, they must have really wanted me and others around me to see them. I am now going to describe some experiences that I had that were so bizarre it caused me to reconsider what these creatures actually are. Two of the incidents I had already spoken about. One was the night I saw the glowing red eyes near the pull-out at Lava Lake, and the other was the glowing eyes on my trail cam inside the truck's cab on Larry's property. What was so interesting was that the red glow looked artificial and overly large. I've seen red eyes on animals in photos, but it was nothing like what I saw. The eyes appeared to be illuminated and did not look like eyeshine. Actually, they did not look anything like eyeshine. The closest thing I could compare them to is when the eyes light up on the mask the aliens used in the Predator movies.

The second inexplicable experience that I had was when I awoke one morning. I had been sleeping on my stomach, and when I opened my eyes, I knew I was being watched. It was exactly the same feeling I had when the male Bigfoot came to my house and watched Nathan and me in our backyard, packing wood. More strangely,

DR. MITCH VERDE, PHD

however, I immediately sensed that I was somehow mentally connected to whoever was watching me. This part of the story is difficult to describe. It was not like I was verbally communicating with him. It was more like I just knew what he was up to. However, I also sensed that he could not know what I was thinking and feeling. I refer to him as a he because after I sensed something was watching me, information flooded my mind. I instantly knew that whatever was watching me was a male, and it was directly above me. In addition, I sensed that he was a young male and moreover, that he had been watching me for some time and was growing bored by it. In fact, I sensed that he was no longer paying attention and was looking elsewhere, daydreaming, or dozing off. I realized that since the feeling of being watched was the same feeling I had when the patriarch Bigfoot was watching my son andme on our property, I concluded that it must be a Bigfoot and that it was the adolescent son. Now, it occurred to me to just stay there and not move. However, I was intrigued by this experience and wanted to see if it was all in my head. For a second, I imagined I would turn over and look at some disembodied Bigfoot head hanging in the air and staring down at me. I also considered that I may turn over and see nothing. However, when I weighed the probability, I concluded I was about to see something. I made this conclusion because I could still feel this mental, almost physical connection to this thing. In one quick movement, I quickly spun over onto my back, and no, there wasn't a disembodied Bigfoot head. However, to my amazement, a perfectly circular light was on the ceiling directly above me. It looked as if someone was holding a flashlight near the ceiling. However, the light had a yellow tinge to it. As I looked at the light, I again felt that he was not paying attention and had a stronger impression that he was daydreaming. I began counting, and at the count of three, I sensed that he became startled after realizing I was looking at him. I had bamboo blinds on my window, and the blinds let in two slits of light that shone on my ceiling near the corner of the room. I could still sense its emotions and feelings, and after, he was initially startled and somewhat scared that I was looking at him. I could sense his mind scrambling for what to do, almost as if he felt trapped. The circle of light then moved in a straight line directly towards the slits of light coming through the blind and then briefly stopped about half an inch from the slits of light. I could sense that he was purposefully doing this, but I had no clue why he was doing it. Then amazingly, the circle of light moved into one of the slits and changed its shape to hide within the light coming through the blinds. Furthermore, I could sense that he felt relieved because he had found a hiding place. Then, the mental connection I had with him was gone. The experience really threw me for a loop. I thought it was a Bigfoot because of how I felt it thinking, which was very human-like. It also displayed the characteristics of a Naxno<u>k</u> or spirit being. That wasn't my conclusion of the encounter, however. I concluded that it was using some type of advanced technology and that it was not just watching me but that the light was recording me! I got up, pretty pumped up by what just happened. As I started walking towards the bedroom door, I heard a loud scraping sound behind me that startled me. I have a king-size bed with a heavy sley-bed frame, and something moved it a couple of inches across the floor. I looked behind me and saw nothing. But it felt pretty creepy like it was on the other side of my bed, but I just couldn't see it. From this experience, I realized that I didn't know anything about these creatures. People have often reported light orbs associated with Bigfoot, and these stories go back in history before Aboriginal Peoples' contact with Europeans. I have never seen an orb of light, and I don't know if what I saw that day would qualify as a light orb. I was also hesitant to believe some of the stories around some kind of telepathic connection people claimed to have had with Bigfoot. I mean, as far as what I thought that a telepathic connection would be, this was nothing like what I had imagined. So, on the one hand, I thought that they could somehow manifest themselves in a type of light source, have a telepathic connection with people, and somehow appear invisible to our eyes. While these may seem like spiritually connected characteristics, I did not believe that. I now firmly believed that what I just experienced was one of them using several of their technologies. And the telepathy, I don't know if you would call that technology or an artifact of being so close to a Bigfoot.

While working in Gitwinksihlkw, my coworkers showed me a picture taken in local gymnasium on a cell phone. The person who took the picture was taking a picture of her daughter playing basketball. However, when she looked at the picture, the was a figure moving from her left to right past the field of the photograph. When I saw the picture, I immediately began laughing and told my coworkers that they probably thought it was an evil spirit. They immediately scoffed at me and said I probably thought it was a Bigfoot. I pointed out that the dark figure had very long hair on her head and a tuft of hair was jutting out from the back of her knee. The figure looked to be an adolescent girl, but the woman who took the picture indicated that there was nobody walking past her. I spoke to the nephew of the woman who took the picture and told him that I thought it looked like a Bigfoot. He agreed and told me that while the adults could not see the Bigfoot walking around in the gym, some small children could see it and were terribly frightened by it. If I hadn't seen the picture with my own eyes, I would still not believe Bigfoot could be invisible to human eyes. However, it got me to rethink my experience on the Bigfoot Road with Guy Guy when we were cutting firewood. In terms of physics, the cut end of the log should not have been rising in the air. There were no trails through the thick fireweed to the other end of the log and no movement at the other end whatsoever. Initially, the event made no sense until I saw that photograph and heard that small children could see it and adults could not. I had to conclude the possibility that the male Bigfoot was actually lifting the cut end of the log and that we just could not see him. I'm unsure, nor can I understand how the Bigfoot can do things like appear invisible to us or manifest itself into spheres of light. I only know what I have seen.

This final story will be the hardest for you to believe, and well, I wished I hadn't seen it. I have actually only recently screwed up the courage to start writing this part of the book because it is so incredulous. Remember the community of Gitwinksihlkw, and the story the fellow told me about seeing three Bigfoot walking along the shore of the river. One day, around noon, I left the post-secondary institute where I worked. I was traveling to Smithers to teach a couple of psychology courses. As you go to cross the bridge, you have to slow down so you can see if someone is coming across the bridge because it is only a one-lane bridge. As I neared the bridge, I saw a car coming; a man and a woman were in the front seats. I had already stopped my car near the bridge and was looking straight ahead at the forest away from the bridge when my attention was diverted by a very bright glint of sunlight off to my right behind the approaching vehicle. The glint just appeared and was about ten feet above the bridge, and more remarkably, there was initially nothing there to cause the glint. What I saw next, I was not able to understand. Out of the bright flash of light came a clear circular object slowly flying or floating through the air alongside the bridge and over the river. At first, I couldn't tell its trajectory. However, as it slowly moved, I could see it was not moving parallel to the bridge but at a slight angle away from it. Even more crazy sounding, there was something inside the craft. When I first saw it, looked like there was a large letter X structure inside the sphere, with each end of the X making contact with the sides of the sphere. The X structure appeared to be black. However, as the sphere moved closer to the forest near the end of the bridge, I could see that it wasn't an X shape made of some solid material; some creature seemed to be bracing itself inside the clear sphere. It had its hand stretched out to brace itself, and it had its feet stretched out as well. I could see what appeared to be its head bent downwards, and I thought it was going to lift its head and look at me, but it did not. The sphere slowly moved into the treetops atop the rock cliff and disappeared. While I definitely thought it was a Bigfoot in there, the whole reference point of something inside a clear-moving sphere basically didn't give me enough information to be positive. Although it was fairly close to me, I did not even notice if it was hairy. By the time it reached the tree tops, the car was about thirty to forty feet from the end of the bridge, and I began looking at the driver's eyes to see if he seemed surprised by anything. He pulled off the bridge and drove past me, and neither he nor his passenger seemed like anything was out of the ordinary. I quickly drove onto the bridge and looked into my side view mirror but could not see the sphere. Now, even if it wasn't a Bigfoot inside this thing, it's still an amazing thing to see. I often wondered what it was and whether it had been camouflaged or cloaked, and the mechanism malfunctioned. Or had it been traveling at high speed and only slowed at that point before it entered the forest?

Now I know these stories seem pretty out there, but they are true. What the heck are these things? They can't be normal animals. Normal animals don't have artificially illuminated eyes, which I suspect may be night vision goggles. They don't talk or make jokes. They can't appear in the form of light or be mentally connected to people. And for sure, if it was a Bigfoot in that sphere, they can't fly around in unknown aircraft. After I experienced these events first-hand, I began to reinterpret some of the stories people told me. For example, the people in Gingolx who saw Bigfoot tracks leading to the house and only two leading away from the house. Perhaps the Bigfoot simply went invisible or got into an invisible craft and flew off.

In the past few years, when taking breaks from my school work, I would read Bigfoot stories on the internet and watch shows about Bigfoot. I used to think outlandish stories about Bigfoot were totally made up. I watched several interviews with people from different walks of life who claim that they actually saw a Bigfoot disappear. In one case, a fellow claimed that he and two friends also interviewed saw spheres of light surrounding them in the forest. Then, a Bigfoot appeared out of nowhere, began running toward them, and disappeared mid-stride. While none of the three could see it, they could see the leaves moving on the ground and could hear it as it ran past them and, according to one of the interviewees, knocked him to the ground. For several years, I assumed it was like the Spider-Man story, but because several people claimed to have witnessed this invisibility phenomenon, I began to think that maybe people in modern times were actually just experiencing what Indigenous Peoples had experienced in past times.

I came across an interesting documentary on one of my smart TV channels. The documentary was set around a house and cottage in a forested rural area. A man had experienced numerous strange occurrences while living there, which he attributed to Bigfoot. One of the things he had been finding was small human being type figures woven out of twigs. Interestingly, I had seen almost identical figures in a different documentary many years earlier. One interesting part of his story was that while the figures often appeared in the morning and were left on or around his vehicle, they were sometimes placed inside his locked vehicle. He also noticed that something was getting inside the locked cottage and leaving drawings there. I think that in any other context, one might have concluded that the property was haunted.

The fellow had a friend, and together, they began leaving food out what they believed was for Bigfoot. They had a particular tree where they would leave fruit and goodies, and the food was always taken by the next morning. At the end of the documentary, they loaded up the tree with food and placed a microphone nearby. The men stayed in a tent a short distance away and, possibly after a few beers, began singing. Then, the recording from the microphone was played. At first, you could hear the food being removed from the tree. Then, you could hear something talking, and it definitely sounded like a male. The talking or vocalizations were very similar to the Bigfoot recording I have heard in the past. That particular recording that I had heard in the past was computer analyzed by two different credible sources. They independently concluded that the vocalizations were definitely a language, and that the range within the vocalizations was outside of the human ability to make. As the documentary ended, the most amazing thing occurred. The talking turned into singing. I know it is anthropomorphizing, but the singing sounded like he was lonely.

Now I understand that some things about the Bigfoot phenomena seem unbelievable, and I do not contest that. In addition, the lack of a physical body or skeleton bolsters the Skeptic's position that Bigfoot does not exist. But what if physical specimens do exist, but there are some efforts on the part of Governments to cover it up? There are some stories out there and some personal experiences that suggest there is a concerted effort to keep this information from the public.

I came across a couple of online stories that stood out for me. Both stories had to do with the military and Mt. St. Helens. In one story, a fellow in the military was put in charge of watching several piles of dead animals being retrieved and piled. At some point, others came and began burning the piles. This happened to all the piles of animals such as bear and elk. However, one pile of animals was covered by large tarps. At some point, these animals were put in nets and taken away by helicopter. While the individual was sworn to secrecy, at some point, he divulged that the animals that were covered by the tarps were Bigfoot.

The second story I came across was even more incredulous. A man in the US Air Force was on his way to Victoria, BC, in Canada, to do some cross-training with the Canadian Air Force. On their way, they were stopped by US military personnel and told they were being put on another assignment. They were re-routed to a place near Mt. St. Helens and brought to a military medical clinic set up in the forest. When they asked what they were doing there, they were told to guard the camp. Every once in a while, a vehicle would arrive with extremely tall people wearing hoodies and trench-coats. The fellow said that he never saw the faces of the patients being brought into the medical tents. This went on for a couple of weeks.

After a couple of weeks had passed, a helicopter landed nearby, and one of the tall patients exited the tent and walked over to the man who came out of the helicopter. To the fellow, it appeared that the tall man and the man from the helicopter were communicating. The man in the helicopter then gave orders to one the senior military people on site. The next day, a military truck pulled up, and several of the men, including the fellow who told this story, were told to get into the back of the truck, as did the tall guy. At some point during this ordeal, he realized the tall guy wasn't a man but a Bigfoot. They traveled for some distance, and the Bigfoot signaled for them to stop the truck. He got out and called into the forest, or what was left of the forest. There was a call back, and he and some soldiers went to look.

From what the fellow said, they found another Bigfoot, but he was in bad shape. The injured Bigfoot communicated with the other Bigfoot, and then the Bigfoot walked back to the truck while several soldiers remained behind. A shot rang out, and as the story went, the soldiers shot the critically injured Bigfoot. They drove another distance, and again, the process was repeated. In some cases, there was no response to the Bigfoot calls into the forest. In another case, a Bigfoot did call back. Again, they went in, and while the injured Bigfoot had a badly burned leg, he was deemed to have a chance to make it. They took him into the military truck and transported him back to the military clinic. The next day, the Air Force personnel were brought together and sworn to secrecy over the event. They were transported out of the military clinic that day.

Awareness, belief, knowledge, and understanding. This was the evolution of my thought process around Bigfoot. At first, I was aware of Bigfoot until I watched that show when I was six. When I found that footprint in the apple orchard, I still wasn't sure whether it was a large human-shaped footprint or that of a very large bear. However, that experience did lead me to believe that they might exist. What is interesting about my experiences is that I have rarely concluded initially that I had found evidence of Bigfoot, or even had seen Bigfoot. I usually tried to explain it as something else, and even told myself outlandish things to account for those experiences. If I was so quick to try and disregard my own experiences, I am not surprised that, as a society, we are so quick to write off peoples' Bigfoot experiences to some alternative explanation, even when the alternative explanation is actually more difficult to believe and unsupported by any scientific reference. After many encounters and eyewitness sightings over the years, there is no doubt in my mind that Bigfoot exists. On multiple occasions Bigfoot experiences when others were with me, they will too attest to the experience, although in some cases, we didn't see Bigfoot. But in getting past my knowledge that Bigfoot do indeed exist, I still don't understand what they are.

When I first arrived in Prince George to start my PhD program, I went to look for someone to cut my hair. There was a hairdresser's place near where I lived, and I decided to give it a try. There was a First Nations woman there who happened to be from a nearby valley to where I'm from. As she cut my hair, we began chatting about Bigfoot, and she told me a story of seeing one while she was snowmobiling when she was younger. Then, she told me an incredible story. Two weeks earlier, her brother had phoned her from Vancouver. He was a trucker, and he and another trucker were each driving a rig down to Vancouver. Near Ashcroft, the first trucker hit something large that was crossing the highway and pulled over, thinking he had struck a moose. His partner pulled over as well, and a man driving a white pick-up who was following them also pulled over. When they got to the ditch to see what he had hit, they were shocked to see a large Bigfoot laying in it. Initially, they thought it was dead. They were shocked and frightened and began dragging the Bigfoot out of the ditch and placed it in the bed of the man's white pick-up. Apparently, it woke up and began to make the sound of a mewing cat. They realized it was badly injured, so they dropped it to the Ashcroft Police Department and dropped it off. You can read about this story on the internet. When the officer in charge of the department was contacted, he commented that they don't have a Bigfoot on ice in a cooler in the back and that the only cooler they had was a small one used for specimens they collect.

According to my hairdresser, she called her brother a couple of weeks later to discuss the matter. He became very serious and told her he couldn't discuss it. She asked him why, and he explained that the authorities, he didn't elaborate on who, contacted him and the other truck driver and told them not to talk about it. He didn't elaborate on whether they had been threatened with repercussions if they did.

Some months later, I was looking on the internet to see if there were any Bigfoot researchers in the Prince George area. I came across this guy's name and called him. He indicated that the story on the internet was misleading and that he was not a Bigfoot researcher but had been organizing some kind of Bigfoot community discussion. I explained that I had some pictures of footprints if he was interested and an interesting story for him. He agreed to meet me at a local Tim Hortons, and I asked him to come alone.

I got to the Tim Hortons before him, and although it was busy there, I knew it was him when he entered the store. I waved him over and showed him some pictures on my computer. After about fifteen or twenty minutes, another man came in dressed in a black leather jacket and a black Australian outback hat. I looked at him, turned to the guy I was meeting, and asked if that fellow was with him. He sheepishly looked at me and said that he was. He apologized for bringing someone else, so I waved over the other guy. I began telling him about the story my hairdresser told me. As I neared the end of the story, a grin broke out on his face. I was a little peeved by that and asked him what the hell he was grinning about. He quickly pulled back and stated that his daughter was best friends with the daughter of the trucker who had hit that Bigfoot! The fellow approached the trucker who hit the Bigfoot and phoned him. The trucker became irate and told the fellow that nothing happened. He then threatened the fellow that if he ever called him again, he would contact the RCMP and press charges for harassment. I mean, if the guy did not hit a Bigfoot, why would he react in such a way to a simple phone call?

After finally getting Bigfoot on a trail-cam, I was very excited and showed many people the still frames of the video. I previously spoke to several RCMP members about their Bigfoot sightings in the Nass Valley. They were reluctant to discuss their experiences publicly as they feared the repercussions from the RCMP administration. While I can't divulge the names of the officers, one of them contacted me and warned me that I needed to be careful. The officer indicated that there was indeed a cover-up surrounding the Bigfoot phenomenon. The cover-up, the officer stated, was not just limited to the RCMP but also extended to the higher levels of government. Two days after I spoke with the officer, I began to hear clicking sounds on my telephone. While I am not paranoid, I thought my phone was being tapped. That lasted for about three months and then stopped.

I had the idea to start looking through British Columbia's internet site on the Freedom of Information Act. There are a lot of references to businesses that use the name Bigfoot, so the research was slow and arduous. Finally, I came upon this wildlife report commissioned by the province of BC. Interestingly, the first four pages of the report had been removed. A statement referenced a number explaining why the pages had been removed, but I could never find a number system explaining why data or information would be removed from a public report. More interestingly, however, was that on the page, there was the first sentence of the report. The first sentence of the report was discussing Bigfoot. Several months later, I returned to the same page, and the reference to Bigfoot in the report's first sentence had been removed. Only the reference to the first four pages and the corresponding number that referenced why the pages were removed remained.

At some point, I came across the notion of having Bigfoot crossing signs in the Nass Valley. I decided to do some research, and lo and behold, I came across another piece of information on BC's Freedom of Information site. It was an article in a BC Provincial Newsletter. The article's author was also asking why we wouldn't have Bigfoot crossing signs in BC, particularly at places where there were numerous sightings of Bigfoot crossing highways. One of the people he interviewed was in upper management for the Department of Highways. In their discussion of a particular stretch of highway, the individual from the Department of Highways stated that as a scientific conclusion, Bigfoot does not exist. However, he explained that the BC government had retrieved several specimens of an undiscovered animal. So, it may be that governments have Bigfoot specimens that have been killed in vehicle accidents, volcanos, or other events. Rather than just outright denying it, the fellow from the Department of Highways was using semantics to describe Bigfoot as an undiscovered animal. You can find this interview if you google Bigfoot crossing signs and BC Provincial newsletter.

For a long time, I was arrogant enough to think that it was I who was watching Bigfoot. In reality, acknowledging their mastery in their natural environment has led me to entertain the idea that they have more likely had more experience watching me than me watching them. Why are they so interested in coming around the forest that surrounds our neighborhood? Over time I realized that my property is within their family territory, but some of my experiences were so bizarre that I had to go from concluding that they were flesh and blood creatures that evolved on this earth to accepting that they may be something else entirely. This progression or evolution of thought is not unique to me. There are several Bigfoot documentaries in which Bigfoot experiencers have concluded the same thing. What they have in common with me is that their thought process and conclusions changed over many years of experience. Another common element is that our experiences started with finding basic evidence, then progressed onto sightings of Bigfoot, and then progressed onto experiences that can't be explained with our conventional knowledge about living creatures on this earth. I can't tell you what Bigfoot are. I don't understand what they are, I only saw what they can do. Maybe they are spirit beings, or multi-dimensional beings. I prefer to think they are flesh and blood but have technologies far beyond ours. I'd like to think they evolved here on earth, but my frame of reference for earthly-bound primate species has not allowed me to reach that conclusion. Whatever they are, they are real, and I feel honored to have experienced them and walked alongside the family whose territory my property is located on. Moreover, I am honored to have been able to write this book and present my experiences to the readers. Let us not bicker about who is right in their beliefs about whether Bigfoot exists or not. Let us agree that life can be stranger than fiction and that, as a species in our own right, our collective knowledge makes us who we are. There is no single approach to knowledge, and to believe so, disregards knowledge important to our survival as a species. God Bless.

Dr. Mitch Verde PhD

POST SCRIPT

F ive years ago, I accepted a job in the Chilcotin territory, British Columbia. I had never been to the Chilcotin before and thought of it as an adventure. I signed on as a Community Psychologist in the community of Tl'etinqox and a few months later I accepted the position as Health Director. More recently I was appointed Chief Executive Officer. While parts of the Chilcotin territory encompass the Coast Mountain Range, Tl'etinqox is situated in a semi-desert region, cold in the winter and blisteringly hot in the summer. When I reached the community for the first time, I looked at the large amount of burnt forest, and sparsely treed living forest compared to the Nass Valley, and I wondered if they had Bigfoot here.

It wasn't long before I heard about local Bigfoot stories. One story stood out among several which was about how men from the community tracked, killed, and buried a Bigfoot that they believed had been digging up graves in the local cemetery and taking the bodies away. On a more positive note, there was another story of a man who was hunting moose, and he had a Bigfoot in his rifle sights. After realizing that it was a Bigfoot because the creature had turned to look at him, the hunter lowered his rifle and promptly left the area. The next morning, the hunter who had lived in a nearby cabin, left his cabin early one morning and found a half moose carcass laying in front of his home. He reported that off in the distance three Bigfoot were walking in the opposite direction.

Reports continue to this day about tree knocking, and strange howls and screams coming from the forest around the community. The nurse that worked here when I first arrived had told me that she had been renting a small farmhouse which was located miles off the main highway, and that she would often wake to a new animal skull that was left on her porch. She thought it was a Bigfoot leaving gifts for her.

The organization that funds health services in most BC Indigenous communities holds several conferences a year. One of the things they do at the conferences is to book individuals to provide wellness activities. Things such as massage and the like are common but at one event, I heard that there were a couple of psychics. I was able to get the last available booking for one of the psychics, only for the sake of amusement, or so I thought. It's not that I don't believe psychic abilities exist, I know they do, however I believe that most people who claim to be psychics are not in fact psychics.

As I entered the darkened area of the psychic's bordered off section, I saw a deck of tarot cards on the table. I asked her what they were, feigning ignorance, and she boldly stated, "those are just for show. I don't need them." I found her response most refreshing, and I readily sat down at the table across from her. "You just had a brother who passed away" she claimed.

"No," I responded. Without missing a beat and with confidence she said, "you just had an uncle who passed away, and he called you brother." Previously I mentioned in this book about my uncle Herb who had recently passed away prior to me moving to Tl'etinqox. Herb always called me "wak" the Nisga'a word for brother.

"Yes, I did just lose an uncle who called me brother," I confessed. As the reading progressed, the psychic was quite clear on several other issues that at the time I couldn't confirm nor disconfirm. It was only later that I found out she was bang on target with those things as well. Near the end of the reading, she hesitated and said, "what is this?"

"What is what?" I asked.

"Two Bigfoot just walked out of the forest."

"Two Bigfoot just walked out of the forest?" I questioned eagerly while attempting to conceal my surprise.

"Yes, it can mean that you are close to nature," she remarked, her eyes looking down.

"I know about Bigfoot" I told the psychic." She paused for a few seconds, and then asked me "do you hear them when they talk to you?" I didn't want to seem like I was off my rocker, so I said "no."

"He wants to talk to you" she stated. "He lives in a cave which is high up and difficult to access."

"We don't have caves like that where I come from" I said. "Our territory is heavily forested and while there are caves, you can't see them through the trees."

"It's not where you are from" she stated. "It's where you work, like the rock walls and caves found above Williams Lake." Well, I guess gob-smacked wouldn't have done justice as to how I felt about what she just said. This person had no idea who I was, or even what my name was. I can guarantee you that she couldn't read my signature on the sign-up sheet, and I was a relatively unknown health professional at that time. She then took it even farther, asking me, "what do you call yourself?"

"What do you mean?" I asked.

"Do you call yourself a psychic?" she asked.

"No" I said.

"Do you call yourself a medium?" she asked. Once again, I answered "no." She paused for a second or two, and then her eyes lit up. "Are you a Shaman?". I looked into her eyes at this point, and before I could say a word, she said, "Yes, that's it, you are a Shaman."

"Well," I said, "Shaman in Russian translates as 'the one who knows' and I do know some things about Bigfoot, and some things about spirituality." I thanked her very much and while it appeared that she wanted to talk more, my curiosity was satisfied, and felt I got more out of the reading than I had anticipated.

When Marie and I first moved to Tl'etinqox, we were placed in the Blue Drop Motor Inn, otherwise known locally as the Blue House. When we arrived at the house and first opened the door, I placed my left foot through the door's threshold and then immediately put my arm out and in front of Marie's chest. "Don't come in I exclaimed, there is something here."

"A ghost?" she asked.

"Yes", I responded." After a minute or so, I could sense that it wasn't anything threatening so we went inside. It still hadn't been cleaned but strangely I immediately recognized the inside of the Blue House. You see, three years earlier, I had what I call an e-dream. Others may refer to these types of dreams as a premonition dream. They are qualitatively different from regular dreams because while dreaming, I am fully aware that that what I am experiencing in the dream will occur later in the future. In fact, I knew that the place I had dreamt of would be in the community where I would be working after completing my PhD. While dreaming, I even questioned the cosmos as to why I would be living in such an accommodation if I had a PhD. I then realized in my dream that that this is where I was going to be sent, and that it was the place where I was "supposed" to be working in the future.

We came back to the Blue House after a couple of hours and found the housekeeper cleaning the home. We stood at the bottom of the doorway and asked her what was up with the house. At first, she sheepishly claimed nothing, but after I assured her that we would not say anything nor tell anyone that she mentioned anything, she blurted out, "It's haunted!" She began telling us stories and described how sometimes after she finished making a bed, she would leave the room and upon returning, the bed would be messed up again. She also indicated that the last person who stayed there, ran out in the middle of the night in her underclothes with only a blanket wrapped around her. Iterations of the latter story were later told to me from several people, along with many other tales of the Blue House.

We slept in the living room the first night with the lights on. The house was alive with knocks, creaks and bangs coming from every corner. Although there was no second floor, we could hear distinct footsteps across the ceiling, which were quite unnerving. Sometimes, you would see a dark shadow darting from the bathroom, across the kitchen, and through the door of the closest bedroom. The morning after our first night, I was sitting in my car with the door still open and a friendly German Shepherd stuck his head in and put his chin on my lap. As I was petting him, I had an idea. I took him inside and led him upstairs, which he quite enjoyed, evidenced by his running around excitedly. I then took him downstairs by the collar, and two steps into the basement, he lowered his head to within a few inches of the floor and his tail moved between his legs. Aha! Now I knew where this spiritual presence was focused, I thought to myself.

The basement was in bad shape due to past flooding and was dirty and smelled of mold and mildew. Although we avoided going downstairs, we stayed at the Blue House for four and a half months and the washer and dryer were down there so we couldn't avoid the basement entirely. Apparently, the Blue House had been where priests had lived in past years, and the last priest who lived there had died in the home and was found on the kitchen floor halfway between the bathroom and the closest bedroom. More eerily, he already had his coffin stored in the basement. I don't think I have to tell you how happy we were when the trailer that we now live in became available. I did wonder however, the night before we moved into the trailer, was the psychic right about this local Bigfoot wanting to communicate with me? I thought to myself, if he did, there would be no better time to make his presence known than on our first night living in the trailer.

Our first day in the trailer was a relief. The trailer was less than a year old, and quite honestly, was the newest place I had ever lived in, and we even had a dishwasher! At the same time however, I was half expecting something to happen, even though I sensed that there were no spirits in the trailer. Somewhat on cue, Marie called me into the living room and said that she heard fingernails scratching and tapping on the main living room window. I looked out the window expecting to see a horse, but nothing was there. I tried to reassure her that it was probably a horse rubbing up on the windowsill. I had this feeling however, that because the scratching and tapping sound was coming from a height of around seven feet off the ground, perhaps the psychic's revelation that a local Bigfoot wanted to communicate to me had some merit.

Last year, one of our employees showed me some pictures of what appeared to be large Bigfoot tracks near the tree line across from the community cemetery. She counted 23 in total, and the tracks were a stone's throw away from the trailer that I currently live in. Last winter, I was in the washroom, and I heard something knocking on the outside of the trailer, and the sound was coming from behind the mirror, which I keenly perceived because I was looking in the mirror at the time. The height of the mirror measured from the ground outside is between eight to nine feet. When I walked out of the bath-room, Marie asked me what the sound was. I told her that it was something outside knocking on the trailer. I then texted Cecil who had moved into the Blue House, and Gabe who lived in a trailer behind our place, because both had a clear line of sight to the trailer, but neither of them saw anything outside our trailer. My son Nathan and I then went out for a look, however there were no people or animals, and no tracks in the fresh snow.

A couple of days later I was sitting in the living room alone, and I heard fingertips and fingernails tapping on one of the two living room windows that were only a few inches below the ceiling. Marie called out to me from the bedroom and asked what that strange noise was, and I told her that someone was tapping on one of the living room windows. Somewhat disconcerting though, was the fact that those windows are roughly ten feet off the ground. I only texted Gabe that time because Cecil had no view of the backyard and Gabe once again said that she couldn't see anyone in the yard. Nathan and I went outside but were once again unable to find any tracks in the snow. In the past, when strange things like this happened to me, it usually occurred indoors. The Nisga'a sometimes refer to it as "Nigit", which is a spirit that comes around just prior to, or just after someone in the family passes away. We have 160 people in our sub-house of Gwingyoo, and over 800 people in the House of Duuk'. I've experienced a lot of Nigit in my life, way too much Nigit! Three days after the fingertips on the window event, I was informed that one of my nieces had passed away. Now, I wasn't sure whether it was a Nigit, or whether a Bigfoot was trying to get my attention. The fact that the knocking and tapping was eight to ten feet off the ground and was coming from the outside suggested it may have been a Bigfoot, and the observation that there were no tracks wasn't entirely surprising to me based on what I had previously experienced in the Nass. I can tell you one thing however, that I'm not going to climb up to any caves to look for him, and there are numerous caves located within the rock walls in the cliffs behind our trailer. I indicated earlier in this book that some people think that Bigfoot and spirits are from the same source. I have reserved my opinion about that, but I have heard many stories in which Bigfoot are viewed around cemeteries. In Nisga'a culture, and other Indigenous cultures, it is said that Bigfoot choose the people who are allowed to see them, which I kind of do believe now. My cousin once introduced me to someone as "Mitch is the man who walks with Sasquatch," and while I found that somewhat comical, people in the Nass do seek me out to tell me their stories.

While I thoroughly enjoyed completing this book on Bigfoot, I had also began writing another book around the same time I had started writing this book. My second book will be titled "The Secret of Life in a Paper Bag." The book is comprised entirely of personal stories of what I call e-experiences or extraordinary experiences, and my thoughts around those experiences. It is not unlike the approach I used in this book; however, the topic is different, but in a way may be related. I will describe one such experience to you now, only if to whet your appetite. A month or so after arriving in the Chilcotin, I was at work and saw a poster for a local rodeo on the poster board. I had never been to a live rodeo and so was looking at the date and location of the event. As I read the information on the poster, the center section of the poster appeared to move out towards me, as if in

3D, and then sprang back, bounced in and out again before reverting to being flat again. It was like ripples on water if one dropped a stone in it. The only comparison I could make was the special effects in the movie "Matrix". Now I knew that the event had only occurred in my mind, and that the poster hadn't changed from two dimensions to three and back again, but it was quite a cool perception. While I had experienced many unusual things before, I had never had an e-experience quite like this one. However, as the poster appeared to become flat again, my eyes settled on the raffle prizes, and more specifically, the second prize of $2,500. I instantly knew, without any doubt, that I was to win the second prize at the rodeo raffle! Moreover, I knew that the raffle prize was a gift, a sort of bonus for embracing my cosmic "assignment" to the Chilcotin.

The day of the rodeo came, and Marie didn't really want to go. I didn't want to go alone, and through some persuasion, including me telling her that we couldn't pass up the raffle prize, and that it was a type of cosmic bonus for us coming to work in the Chilcotin, she agreed to go. The first thing we did upon arriving at the rodeo was to purchase four raffle tickets. I was so excited because I hadn't won a raffle for so much money before, I was telling my co-workers at the rodeo that I was going to win the second-place prize. A few hours later we purchased two more tickets and had six in total. I held them in front of me, and looked at the numbers, and knew which ticket was the winner. I put the other five tickets in one pocket, placed the winning ticket in the other and went to sit on the bleachers opposite the announcer's stage. I told the other people sitting on the stand that I had the winning ticket for the second-place prize, and although most just chuckled, a couple of them had puzzled looks on their faces realizing that it looked like I believed what I was saying. There were five thousand tickets sold, and some lucky person won the ATV which was the first prize. After announcing the first-place prize, I pulled out my ticket, briefly waved it so the others in the bleacher could see, and then held it high in my left hand. I clenched my right hand into a fist, and held it low to my side, and honestly, the only thing I was thinking at the time was hoping the announcer didn't butcher the pronunciation of my name. He didn't, and as he read my name, I yelled something like, "Yesssssss" as I dropped my left hand and thrust my right fist into the air. When I turned around, there was a look of confusion on several of the peoples' faces.

In this book, I provided my observations after each Bigfoot experience, which is a similar approach I will take in my future book. Human life is so rich in experience, and our collection of rich experiences does not have to reside in a box defined by cultural bias. Human experience just is, and although we interpret those experiences through a culturally subjective lens, there is an objective reality out there, currently outside of our cognitive grasp. We don't know what we don't know, and I'm OK with that, and I hope you are too, and if, or when you read my future book, I hope that you find the stories enlightening, encouraging, and heart-lifting. Thank you so very much for reading Misty Giants of the Lava Bed. From the bottom of my heart, I appreciate it, hope you enjoyed it, and I commend your patience while reading Bigfoot tales from the Nass Valley, documented by The World's Worst Sasquatch Researcher. Once again, God bless.

Dr. Mitch Verde (PhD)

AFTERWORD

Go to hangarıpublishing.com to learn more about the Authors and stay up to date with their newest releases.

www.ingramcontent.com/pod-product-compliance
Lightning Source LLC
Chambersburg PA
CBHW071148120626
46546CB00006B/2167